D0427544

Doing Business in Mexico

Jay M. Jessup and Maggie L. Jessup

Prima Publishing
P.O. Box 1260BK
Rocklin, CA 95677
(916) 632-4400

Production by Melanie Field, Bookman Productions
Composition by WESType
Interior design by Judith Levinson
Jacket by The Dunlavey Studio

Library of Congress Cataloging-in-Publication Data

Jessup, Jay.
  Doing business in Mexico / Jay and Maggie Jessup.
    p.   cm.
  Includes index.
  ISBN 1-55958-277-4 : $21.95
  1. Mexico—Commerce—Handbooks, manuals, etc.
  I. Jessup, Maggie. II. Title.
HF3237.J47   1992
658.8'48'0972—dc20   92-30484
                                     CIP

94 95 96 RRD 10 9 8 7 6 5 4

Printed in the United States of America

How to Order:

Quantity discounts are available from the publisher, Prima Publishing, P.O. Box 1260BK, Rocklin, CA 95677; telephone: (916) 632-4400. On your letterhead include information concerning the intended use of the books and the number of the books you wish to purchase.

CONTENTS

FOREWORD

The Age of North American Continentalism in the *global village* is upon us. The technological revolution has greatly enhanced our capacity to transfer ideas, people, goods, and capital across national boundaries, thereby accelerating regional interdependency. Heralded by the Information Age, the impending economic integration of Mexico, the United States, and Canada indicates a strong need to address the business opportunities and challenges framed in the concept of a *single North American competitive space*. Intense global competition in the world marketplace is painting a clear picture: if American businesses intend to grow and flourish, they must seriously consider doing business in foreign markets.

Information is the key. Small business owners often cite the lack of available information on exporting as their single greatest obstacle to entering the world trade arena. To address this problem, the Jessups have drawn on their rich experience, knowledge, and expertise in the area of United States/Mexico trade to effectively research and write *Doing Business in Mexico*. The authors wisely assume a practical, step-by-step, hands-on approach in this invaluable guidebook that is rich in resources for all those interested in the phenomenal business opportunities awaiting them in both Mexico and Canada. Pragmatic in nature, this book clearly outlines the current, expanding commercial opportunities existing between Mexico and the United States as new technologies and products emerge in the North American marketplace.

This book is a vast resource base of information designed to facilitate business opportunities in Mexico; however, it transcends the usual checklist approach by providing overviews of the economies of Mexico and Canada and, more importantly, by providing insights into cultural idiosyncracies that often impede successful business transactions and growth. The Jessups present their readers with a vision of Mexico, offering invaluable insights on how one can do effective business in Mexico. After a discussion of what new markets lie south of the border, *Doing Business in Mexico* targets trends in specific industries, demonstrating the book's current and up-to-date nature. The practical checklist of *Getting Started* is a veritable roadmap for exploring new business horizons in Mexico, and the ensuing suggestions for pitfalls to avoid have a realistic, practical, and sometimes humorous approach.

The authors wisely include a chapter entitled *Importing Opportunities for Individuals Starting Small*. The pages are imbued with enlightening and encouraging advice and news about breaking into the Mexican market. Here, as in other chapters, the Jessups effectively discuss important legal considerations, the challenges of distribution, pricing, and market research, among other topics.

Looking ahead to the impending economic integration of the Big Three in North America, the Jessups include a timely chapter called *Special Opportunities for Canadians*. Here they draw a positive picture of the changing trade relationship between the United States and Canada as a result of the 1989 Free Trade Pact and discuss the potential business markets that will be open to Canadians interested in extending commercial ties to Mexico. Citing specific examples in the areas of telecommunications, tourism, transportation, manufacturing, banking, and others, the authors clearly indicate the new movement by Canadian businesses to establish strong commercial ties with Mexico in this era of regional interdependency.

The appendixes of *Doing Business in Mexico* constitute a veritable gold mine of practical information designed to make the reader's initial efforts to establish business contacts more effective and profitable. The authors outline the major important companies and franchises in Mexico, provide basic but necessary information about the Mexican government and the country, and list the maquiladoras by city. The Resource Guide generously complements the contents of the book, providing excellent starting points for all those interested in establishing commercial ties with Mexico.

American industry has been going through an unprecedented period of renovation, computerization, and modernization. *Doing Business with Mexico* by Jay and Maggie Jessup effectively shows businesspeople how to take advantage of these advancements and earn the greater profits available from a broader market involvement with our neighbor south of the border, Mexico.

Dr. James P. McCormick, Director
North American Studies Project
Regional and Continuing Education
California State University, Sacramento

Acknowledgments

We would like to thank:

U.S. Department of Commerce

U.S. Department of Agriculture

President Carlos Salinas de Gotari of Mexico and his
administration

Secretaria Particular Andres Massieu

Mexican Secretariat of Ecology and Urban Development

Mexican Government Tourism Office

National Fund for the Development of Tourism
(FONATUR)

Mexican Foreign Investment Commission

Governor Ann Richards, Texas, with special thanks to
Letticia Vasquez

Governor Toney Anaya, New Mexico

American Chamber of Commerce

Hon. Jose Angel Pescador, Mexico's Consul General in Los
Angeles

Hon. Teodoro Maus Reisbaum, Mexico's Consul General in
Atlanta

President George Bush and staff

Dr. James P. McCormick, California State University,
Sacramento

Kathy Parker, U.S. Small Business Administration,
Washington D.C.

Candice Fuhrman, The Candice Fuhrman Literary Agency

Jennifer Basye and Ben Dominitz, Prima Publishing

Dr. J. F. C. Wirth, Mexico City

Maureen Edwards Stanfield, Vancouver, British Columbia

Susan Huetteman, San Mateo, California

Mr. and Mrs. Robert DePalma, San Clemente, California

And most of all, our parents:

Mrs. Alice McLaren, Laredo, Texas, and Riverside,
California

Mr. and Mrs. Melvin Jessup, Orange County, California

Mr. and Mrs. Donald McLaren, Woodville, Texas

1

CATCH A RISING STAR

NOT JUST ANOTHER PRETTY PLACE

Mexico is one of the world's most naturally beautiful countries. Its breathtaking, abundant, accessible, affordable, and picturesque landscapes make it an ideal vacation spot.

The Mexican government has spent millions developing the country's tourism industry. Consequently, we picture Mexico as a vacation hot spot for fun in the sun and dancing until dawn—a place where you can lie back with a tropical drink, read your favorite book, and watch picture-perfect sunsets over an incredibly blue ocean; a place with hundreds of miles of white-sand beaches and nearby marketplaces stretching as far as the eye can see, where vendors wave their wares with outstretched arms and await friendly bargaining. The Mexico most tourists see is a place where life is easy, people are friendly, and children are happy.

1

Mexico's reputation as a vacation paradise is well deserved, but there is also a sophisticated culture and an amazingly advanced economic system beneath the surface. Mexico is now the United States' third largest trading partner. Tens of billions of dollars worth of goods pass across the border between our countries each year, and the figures keep increasing dramatically. Fiscal policies of the late 1980s and early 1990s have brought significant economic stability to Mexico; privatizations, debt restructuring, and enhanced trade have streamlined the business climate. This streamlining, along with a considerable reduction in restrictions on foreign investment and trade, has created new opportunities for informed U.S. and Canadian companies and individuals.

In addition to the economics, the character of the Mexican people makes so much possible. They work long and hard and take great pride in what they do, whether their business is weaving intricate rugs or producing automobiles that set new standards for quality. The U.S. businessperson who understands and can direct this can-do work ethic will be able to take greater advantage of the opportunities we outline in this book. Business opportunities abound in Mexico. The place is Mexico and the time is now for superprofits in the 1990s. The decision to take the first step is yours. The door is wide open.

ECONOMIC MIRACLES

Developments in Mexico since 1988 can only be described as an economic miracle. First we look at Mexico's premiracle economic situation so you can see how it all began. Next we consider the bold plan Mexico's government devised to transform Mexico from a collapsed and stagnating Third World country into an efficient "model" First World economic power. Then we describe how this plan created the unstoppable momentum that Mexico currently enjoys.

Before 1988, overreliance on oil revenues and a subsequent crash in oil prices put Mexico's economy in a dangerous situation. Huge debts piled up as the government borrowed against future production and used the funds to maintain bloated, inefficient, and unprofitable state-run industries. Triple-digit inflation caused great economic instability, and conditions were deteriorating. Economic statism and the resulting protectionist policies made foreign trade and investment prohibitively expensive, with absurdly high tariffs and incomprehensible red tape effectively stopping any inflow of foreign capital.

To make matters worse, Mexicans who still had any money after a series of devaluations sent the money out of Mexico to the United States and other places. The peso was weak, its value crashing along with the national economy. Mexico's disillusioned and scared moneyed class preferred to invest in U.S. dollar accounts. Debt burden and other economic woes left Mexico with no money for maintaining its economic infrastructure; investing in research and development; and maintaining roads, phone systems, and the like. The infrastructure of Mexican business gradually collapsed, leading to record high unemployment. Salaries for bloated and inefficient work forces diverted any possible profits from state-run industries. Furthermore, these industries did not have to worry about competition because they were monopolies, preventing foreign competition from entering the market.

Economic and social matters were bleak; there were just too many problems and no money to fix them.

A new presidential administration took office in 1988, headed by Harvard Business School–educated President Carlos Salinas de Gortari. He and his advisers devised a bold new plan for attacking all these ills at once. Anything less would have been stopgap economic repair, whereas money was needed immediately to generate economic momentum.

Almost simultaneously, several programs were initiated. In the area of foreign trade, protectionist policies were eliminated, tariffs were slashed, and everything possible was done to stimulate foreign trade. Foreign debt payments were restructured, eliminating much of the principal and making payments on the balance manageable. Increased foreign trade and lower debt payments left some money for the government to use to get the ball rolling. At the same time, mass privatization of state-run industries began. Banks, the phone company, and some 1000 other state-run businesses were transferred to the private sector. Billions of dollars were raised, and the industries became more efficient.

Now inflation was the only threat to this newly created momentum. By combining a series of wage and price controls with other economic tools, the government reduced the rate of inflation from 180 percent per year in 1988 to less than 20 percent in the early 1990s.

Salinas' bold plan worked. Inflation slowed, debt restructuring continued, billions of flight capital returned, trade skyrocketed, hundreds of thousands of workers found jobs where none were before, and a new and broader middle class emerged with the new prosperity.

Now with an opportunity to rebuild the entire

country's physical and economic infrastructure, Mexico continued spending millions on public relations so the world could invest in the miracle. As a result, foreign investment increased, more jobs for Mexicans were created, and Mexico's business community became more efficient.

Currently the momentum is self-sustaining and virtually unstoppable. A desperate bluff to solve Mexico's economic woes turned into an economic miracle. Today the world recognizes Mexico as a stable economic power, and investment is flowing into the country. Further stabilization and growth seems sure to continue through the 1990s.

THE WELCOME MAT IS OUT

Currently Eastern Europe and Russia are being touted as "the" place for new markets and tremendous opportunity. However, as just discussed, Mexico too has been accomplishing economic miracles. Although we have been trading with our southern neighbor for centuries, the recent and incredible strides Mexico has taken toward putting its economic house in order have presented us with very tempting opportunities for investment and trade. The welcome mat is definitely out.

In December 1987, Mexico substantially reduced its trade barriers with the United States. Trade between the two countries increased immediately and dramatically. The signing of the United States/Mexico Framework Agreement in 1987, Mexico's joining GATT (General Agreement on Tariffs and Trade) the same year, and passage of the Investment Facilitation Agreement in 1989 all set the stage for unparalleled opportunities.

Tariffs and other restrictions are at an all-time low and are continuing to be reduced. The North American Free Trade Agreement, which could be finalized and in place as early as 1994, promises to be one of the crowning achievements in trade relations between our countries. With the volume of bilateral trade between the United States and Mexico running close to $70 billion per year, there is much excitement in the business community. New policies of free trade, privatization of state-run enterprises, and tight fiscal programs have created tremendous economic momentum. Mexico's government and businesspeople are well aware of what increased trade between the United States and Mexico could mean for their country.

It has never been easier or more profitable to work with our southern neighbors. With proper information, planning, and guidance, a smart U.S. business can easily broaden its market and increase the production/profitability of its product. Mexico has many attractive things to offer a U.S. business. Special programs for U.S. ownership of factories can significantly reduce the cost of production for your product. If you have been thinking of exporting, Mexico's 90 million consumers want U.S. products, and the country's government and big business need our technology and capital goods to rebuild their nation's infrastructure. Investment opportunities abound as restrictions are lifted on foreign ownership of Mexican land and business.

Mexico needs this influx of capital and technology to maintain its economic momentum into the next century. Shrewd U.S. businesspeople can see, however, that these offers are not open to only the United States. Mexico recognizes the United States as an important trading partner but not the only one. It is seeking and obtaining outside investment from many countries—entrepreneurs and corporations worldwide are being offered a window of opportunity and many special incentives for bringing their business into the country.

WHAT TO EXPECT

Roadblocks

Initial inquiries about doing business with Mexico are met with a series of apparent roadblocks. But informed perseverance pays off. One lesson we learned is the importance of distinguishing between "It can't be done" and "I don't know how."

Countless profits have been lost by failing to understand this distinction. Mexican culture is characterized by a great deal of personal pride. In the area of business, pride is sometimes demonstrated to the extreme. Thus, many of the newer opportunities may involve many "It can't be done" responses, so be ready for these obstacles. Persevere, because your uninformed competition may give up at this point. Circumventing the "It can't be done" roadblock will turn problems into steppingstones toward opportunity. We discuss this point in more detail later, but for now carve this lesson in stone!

Need for Help

You need a certain amount of help getting established and learning the ropes. Many resources are available to you (they are discussed in great detail throughout the book); we encourage you to avail yourself of some or all of them.

You need not reinvent the wheel. Probably 95 percent of the problems you will encounter have already been experienced by others. Whether you seek help from the U.S. Commerce Department, other government offices and programs, or an experienced United States/Mexico trade consultant, your search for help will be worth the time and expense. What seems an insurmountable obstacle to you is often an easily dispatched issue for them. You can gain experience the hard way, or you can buy business advice up front. The hard way may be sadly expensive because in Mexico many mistakes cannot be undone, and opportunities once missed may not be regained.

Chapter 5, "Getting Started: A Checklist," will get you through most of your initial research and problem solving. You can do 99 percent of this yourself. Do not be afraid to seek help for that extra 1 percent. You should be well informed about the most cost-efficient and advantageous courses of action available.

Many of the opportunities we outline here require a bold approach. To aggressively seek profits and rewards at this unique historical time, you need a solid plan based on realistic information. Gather your information, prepare your business plan, and have your proposed course of action reviewed by a professional.

As you continue through this book, ideas of your own will arise at every turn. Write them down as they occur to you; they may be the springboard for finding your own niche later on. You can expect much from venturing into the United States/Mexico market. With careful planning, good advice, perseverance, and occasional inspiration, your possibilities for profit are almost limitless.

DISPELLING THE MYTHS

Because Mexico's cultural development and history differ so vastly from our own, a certain mystique surrounds the country, fostering myths, tales, outright lies, and uncertainties. Granted, some might once have had a basis in historical reality, but most negatives that might affect U.S. business are simply not true. Let's separate fact from fiction so your judgment will not be impaired and you will not be discouraged from finding your niche in Mexican trade. Do not lose your opportunity to strengthen economic ties between the United States and Mexico because of an assortment of half-baked stories.

MYTH 1: YOU WILL LOSE YOUR MONEY

Every family includes someone like Uncle Charlie, who has a story for every situation, cautioning the young about life's vagaries. Invariably one of Uncle Charlie's stories is about a friend losing all his money in some venture in Mexico. The story is short on specifics, is hearsay, and probably happened 10 to 50 years earlier, if ever.

From personal experience I know that "Don't take your money to Mexico or you'll lose it!" is simply not true. Mexico is not a lawless, uncharted territory. Hundreds of major U.S. companies are already doing business quite profitably in Mexico, and the number increases daily. In many respects, opportunity and safety are greater in Mexico for U.S. companies than at home.

Hewlett-Packard, Ford, and many others are prosperous models of success.

MYTH 2: CORRUPTION AMONG GOVERNMENT OFFICIALS IS RAMPANT

What about allegations of corruption in Mexico's government? Interestingly, many Mexicans have the same suspicions about the United States as they read about our congresspersons kiting checks, our Savings & Loan scandals, our Wall Street kings being imprisoned. In reality, of course, in both Mexico and the United States, dishonest people and practices are exceptions rather than the rule, which is why they make the news.

Overall, integrity is the order of the day. In the course of doing business with Mexico, we are constantly impressed by the honesty and integrity of the government officials. And they expect and presume the same level of integrity from U.S. businesspeople, so it is incumbent on you and your business associates to live up to this standard.

However, Mexican officials are somewhat different from their counterparts in the U.S. But understanding cultural differences will help you. This guidebook will get you started on the right foot, so you can understand all the levels of interaction that can affect your success in doing business in Mexico. For now, remember that when planning a business in or trade with Mexico, plan for the long run, recognizing that your relationships with the officials involved can determine your success or failure. At the very least, they can affect your profitability. The Mexican government often promotes from within, under their cultural principle of wanting to do business with those they know, respect, and trust. Mexican officials understand that honesty, predictability, and common sense are necessary to turn Mexico into a First World country.

Myth 3: The People Are Lazy and Illiterate

Some myths insinuate that Mexicans are not hard workers, that their education level is low, and that their intelligence does not match ours. Nonsense! The Mexican literacy rate is higher than ours in the United States and still climbing. As to willingness to work, our experience has been that Mexican workers are dedicated to working until the job is done, however long it takes. Mexico's frequent holidays give workers the incentive and stamina to maintain such a pace.

Do not embarrass yourself by presuming to be better educated than the Mexicans. They use every possible opportunity to get more education for themselves and their children. Many Mexicans have advanced degrees from prestigious institutions (often in the United States). The obvious rule is: Do not underestimate the ability of the Mexicans. Mexico is proving itself as its people, business, and government catapult into international commercial preeminence.

Myth 4: Business Associates May Be Dishonest

Some U.S. businesspeople are concerned about becoming involved with dishonest business associates. As a rule of thumb, if you go into Mexico with an "I'm better and smarter than you" attitude, looking to exploit some workers, grab a quick profit, and head back home, you will be fleeced with reckless abandon, and rightly so. At a minimum, you will receive expensive lessons in caution and etiquette because Mexican businesspeople are quite capable of protecting themselves.

Business in Mexico is about the same as it is anywhere. If you are negligent in handling your money, you will lose it; if you think you are smarter than anyone else, you probably aren't. On the whole, business in Mexico is extraordinarily safe. A handshake means more than any contract in the United States, and your carefully chosen business associates will bend over backward to avoid even the appearance of impropriety.

MYTH 5: "I WAS IN TIJUANA BACK IN THE 40s, SO I KNOW MEXICO"

Another cliché is "Heck yes, we used to go down to Tijuana back when I was in the service—I know all about Mexico from that." Although Tijuana is an interesting city with a great deal of commerce, we have found border towns to be a buffer zone of culture clash rather than being representative of either bordering country. In certain respects they almost caricature some elements of their societies.

In any event, never equate a social or even a business visit to a border town with a pervasive knowledge of Mexico and its people. If you base your business decisions on such woefully inadequate information, you may be doomed from the start. Mexico has much, much more to offer, and you should learn as much as possible to take the best advantage of profit opportunities.

MYTH 6: RED TAPE IS EVERYWHERE

Red tape is another stumbling block for many Americans doing business in Mexico. They fear that even when requirements are satisfied, an arbitrary and occasionally capricious government might stop them from moving ahead.

Let's first look at what is involved in doing business in the United States. Even a modest business must have its new employees fill out forms for social security, citizenship, worker's compensation, federal withholding, and more. Employee paychecks include more deductions and adjustments. Quarterly and annual calculations for each employee must be tallied and reported to state and federal governments. Then there are sales taxes, self-employment taxes, occasional inventory taxes, various permits and licenses, corporate filings and formalities, vehicle requirements and the like, and not to mention city, county, state, and federal taxes! And if you call the IRS information hotline, questions are answered correctly only 60 percent of the time. Rules change every year, sometimes retroactively. You are concerned about red tape in Mexico?!

Of course there are rules and requirements in Mexico. But with the proper guidance you should be able to handle your business there with no more red tape than in the United States. Just be sure to follow the rules and comply with the requirements correctly the first time because appeal procedures are somewhat limited and penalties for violating the rules are significant.

To streamline and reduce red tape, the Mexican government has introduced several programs and directives to simplify, make uniform, and speed up applications, rules, and enforcement. It is now much simpler to move goods across the border, and there are strong indications that the trend will continue. Rules for simplifying and reducing time for maquiladora approvals are in the works. Investment rules and regulations are being simplified almost monthly. Once you get started, you may find the regulatory environment in Mexico more congenial than that in the United States. There are actually fewer rules, and those rules are less confusing.

Myth 7: "I Can't Do It, I Don't Know Where to Start"

This attitude will disappear as you read this book. You will know exactly where to start and where to get help. As you enter the world of business in Mexico, you will be in good company. Goodyear, General Motors, McDonald's, and hundreds of other companies are already taking advantage of the country's conducive business environment.

If you represent a large company, there are myriad ways to enhance your profits. If you are an individual or own a small- to medium-sized company, your flexibility is an asset, and even more opportunities will abound. You will have the information on where to start.

New Frontiers

Mexico has emerged from the developmental Dark Ages and entered a new frontier. In the physical sense, "frontier" conjures up an image of vast areas of land and resources not yet put to their best use. In the developmental sense, the word suggests a vision of great economic and cultural voids. The new Mexican frontier encompasses both concepts, and this book was written to help enable you to venture into these new territories.

Mexico's physical frontier consists of its vast areas of undeveloped land. Almost all the country's development has taken place in and immediately around its ma-

jor cities and borders, for two reasons: availability of jobs
has caused migration to the cities and a more deeply
rooted cultural concept of togetherness has discouraged
population dispersion. Even when land just outside a
city can be purchased for very few dollars per acre, a
Mexican citizen will live in incredibly cramped quarters
in the city, to be "where the action is." Lack of significant mass transit also makes living far from the cities
less feasible. Between the major cities, hundreds of thousands of acres are available for development. Ironically,
this land is frequently near (if not on top of) significant
natural resources and dramatic beauty.

The Mexican government and its people are feeling
the crunch of uncontrolled urban development and its
attendant problems and costs. Now programs offer incredible incentives to those willing to develop Mexico's
physical frontier. An acquaintance of ours, a producer of
high-quality wool, outdistanced his competitors by buying a vast area of land five hours outside Mexico City.
From nothing, he and his associates have created a re-
markable, self-sustaining community. Raising sheep
and cattle, and farming to produce the community's
food, his operation requires no outside support from
metropolitan suppliers. Our friend owns a large amount
of land and has created a beautiful and healthful environment for the company, its workers, and their families. And he has done all this for the same price that his
competitors pay to lease small inner-city facilities.

Now that restrictions on land ownership have been
significantly reduced, this kind of opportunity is also
available to U.S. businesses. Perhaps it is time for you to
consider the benefits of taming Mexico's physical frontier.

Mexico's developmental frontier provides opportunities of staggering scope. Until recently, Mexico

survived mainly within its own borders. In other words, it had restrictive policies on importing outside goods, technology, and capital. Although designed to protect Mexico from foreign predators, those policies merely stunted the country's growth, holding Mexico back while other countries developed more global economies. Mexico's new policies embrace the global concept. Whereas Mexico has been lacking developmentally, constrained by limited natural resources, technology, and capital, the lifting of restrictions has created new frontiers of opportunity. From technology to agriculture, from transportation to mining, and across the entire spectrum of a sizable economy, unlimited possibilities await those with the knowledge and willingness to participate.

So much has already been done in the United States that it is difficult for a new company to find its niche. And existing companies looking to new areas can accomplish little in the competitive U.S. economy. Meanwhile, a mere stone's throw from our border stand 100 million consumers eager for U.S. goods, an entire country that needs capital goods to rebuild its infrastructure, and all the land you could possibly want.

PIONEERING SPIRIT

U.S. history and culture are filled with heroes who tackled and tamed new frontiers of land, scientific development, economy, and business. From Daniel Boone to Armand Hammer, from the 49ers to Getty, from Edison to Crocker, most of our great heroes were pioneers of some sort. They opened new areas, found new directions, and formed new companies.

The United States has always been a land where an individual could start with an idea, and with perseverance that idea could spawn a Ford Motor Company, a Microsoft, or an Apple. But can you name three truly great pioneers in the United States in the past 10 or 20 years? They probably got their start 30, 40, or 50 years ago. Although the pioneering spirit has deep roots in our culture and history, of late it has been stifled by our increasingly organized, automated, and corporatized economy. Few frontiers are left to attack, and new ideas are held back by government regulation, sometimes unreasonable union demands, and lack of venture capital. The few companies with sufficient resources to explore new fields in the United States are limited by law from too much pioneering, for fear that their corporate directors will become personally liable.

But rest easy. The pioneering spirit that made this country great is still alive and well—south of our border. United States business is responding to the Mexican government's incentive programs to make pioneering profitable. Reasonably priced, hard-working labor is increasing profitability. The labor unions in Mexico do not have the same expectations as their U.S. counterparts. And Mexican workers appreciate a work opportunity, take pride in their work, and have a lower cost of living; their unions operate on the principles of collective bargaining and basic fairness.

Now U.S. business is manufacturing in Mexico, importing Mexican goods, and opening offices and subsidiaries at a record pace. The trend is away from the corporate gridlock of the United States to Mexico, where the innovator and the improvisor are still welcomed and rewarded. If you have the pioneering spirit, you can build your dreams at a reasonable cost. The U.S. dollar goes a long way in Mexico. Learn from the past, and take advantage of today's opportunities. Note that these opportunities are quite possibly once in a lifetime and thus should be considered privileges not to be abused. Build for the long run, not for the fast profits of a carpetbagger, and Mexico will reward you beyond your dreams.

DIVERSIFYING YOUR RISKS

A recent study of the 1500 largest U.S. companies found that almost half are planning to expand their activities outside the country in the next 12 months. For some companies, this means heading for the newly expanded European market; for others, it means going into the already quite-developed Pacific Rim trading area; and for some, it means heading to Mexico for new opportunities. Many of the corporate giants are opening new facilities and expanding existing ones because they know that diversifying risks is good business.

One important reason for selecting Mexico over other areas is its proximity to the United States. Would producing your product in Hungary really be safe? Are you really diversifying your risks by shipping your product from the Orient on a ship that can take as many as 30 days just to reach your U.S. port? Logic dictates that you would be wiser staying within 2 or 3 hours of your investment and 24 hours of its distribution. Stabilizing your foundation, increasing your safety, and spreading out your assets are what diversifying risks is all about.

Another important issue to consider is Mexico's present willingness to accept foreign investment. With Mexico's low-cost labor pool and enticing incentives, why select the uncertainties of a new Europe or the increasingly restrictive environment of the Pacific Rim? In each case, the uncertainties outweigh any possible benefits, making Mexico the best place to diversify your risks.

Consider the following scenarios and decide for yourself the advantages of looking south:

SCENARIO A

You are already manufacturing in the United States. You elect to produce part of your product in Mexico. In the event of a U.S. labor strike or plant shutdown, you have the option of stepping up production at your Mexico facility during what could be months of negotiations.

SCENARIO B

Your U.S. supplier has labor, credit, or raw material problems. You already have an additional supplier producing part of your requirements. You need only increase your capacity on the Mexico side to weather the storm. The U.S. supplier's problems will not bring about your demise.

These are just two examples of the countless situations in which your foresight might save the day.

For years the Mexican government has been trying to raise the economic standard of living of its people, principally through industrialization. The recent easing of its debt burden, the privatization of key industries, and the introduction of programs favoring foreign investment are all geared toward creating jobs and a good standard of living for Mexico's rapidly growing population. Mexico

has the need and willingness to accept foreign investment with open arms. You want to diversify your risks
and build additional foundations for your business. An
economic marriage between the United States and Mexico could lead your business to success.

Do your homework, and you may find that Mexico
is your answer. Get some answers from this book and
your research; learn to spot opportunities and avoid
problems. Study your competition and analyze their directions. Learn about free trade programs and policies.
In any event, ensure your safety by diversifying your
risks and increasing your profits.

JAPAN AND MEXICO

Most of this book focuses on forming and expanding
relationships between Mexican, U.S., and some Canadian businesses. No such study would be complete without reviewing the positions of another world player,
Japan, the world's second largest buyer of Mexican
products.

In 1988, Japan and Mexico celebrated their 100th
anniversary of formal diplomatic ties and trade. As a
direct result of such trade, many institutions have flour-
ished, including the Bank of Tokyo, whose Mexico City
office has been established for 33 years. In all, 15 banks
have offices in Mexico, including the Export-Import
Bank of Japan and JETRO (Japanese External Trade
Organization). Reciprocally, Bancomer, one of Mexico's
largest banks, has operated in Tokyo for 19 years. Mexico's primary export to Japan is oil. Japan has pur-

chased more than 10 percent of Mexico's crude oil production over the past five years.

Mexico also enjoys direct Japanese investment representing some 5 percent of all foreign trade investment in Mexico. The main areas of Japanese investment are in the maquiladora facilities along the border. Sony, Hitachi, Matsushita, and Toshiba are all represented, arguably making the Mexican border area the television capital of the world. The primary nonmaquiladora Japanese investor is Nissan, with more than half of all Japanese investment. Since it makes an additional $400 million investment to produce cars for the Latin American market, Nissan is prospering with Mexico's economical labor force.

Whereas Japan has excelled in many culturally diverse Asian markets, Japanese companies characteristically have had difficulties adapting to some of Mexico's cultural idiosyncrasies. Exceptionally cautious because of losses on debt under the Brady plan and some miscalculations in their steel dealings, most Japanese companies are trailing the United States, Britain, Germany, and other countries in Mexican investment.

Watch this hesitancy change through the 1990s as, to prove their quality, Nissan has its Mexican plants produce cars for export to Japan. Furthermore, changes in policy that previously limited foreign ownership in Mexican companies to 49 percent should cause a continuous and dramatic increase in Japanese investment.

Beyond all doubt, the United States is and will be in a better competitive position than Japan. A shared 2000-mile border and years of seniority in Mexican investment give the United States a decisive edge.

READYING FOR THE FUTURE

Recent years have brought incredible progress to Mexico. Inflation has been tamed, the unemployment rate has dropped, the government and economy have been streamlined, foreign debt has been reduced, and much more. But Mexico's leaders are not merely sitting back and enjoying their accomplishments; government and business continue to work together toward an even better Mexico. Money that was raised from privatizing industry, increasing foreign trade, and encouraging foreign investment is being used intelligently. Mexico's social and economic infrastructure are being rebuilt as an investment in the future.

Far from resting on their laurels, Mexican leaders are continuing their tight fiscal policies. They are seeking even more foreign trade and permanent investment in Mexico's growth. Programs to improve the environment are underway, and the government is working to secure more and better jobs for Mexico's people.

Our southern neighbor is building a first-rate world economy—globally interactive and socially aware. Mexico's leaders are planning ahead for continuing prosperity into the next century. Wise and informed U.S. businesses are joining the program, heading for Mexico, and readying for the future. Read on to learn how your company can find and participate in these new opportunities.

2

IMPORTANT CULTURAL IDIOSYNCRASIES

All international business requires some degree of cross-cultural awareness. For the U.S. or Canadian businessperson seeking to conduct business in Mexico, such sensitivity is critical. Our countries may be close together physically, but culturally there are fundamental differences. Study these differences, conduct yourself as a culturally prepared businessperson, and you will enjoy success in business in Mexico.

Multinational businesses know that training in the ways of the "host culture" is necessary for problem-free communication in business. They spend hundreds of thousands of dollars preparing their personnel for intercultural business exchanges. The fundamental principle is that business is *not* conducted in a vacuum. People conduct trade and negotiations. People decide with whom they will do business and on what terms. When interpersonal business becomes cross cultural, it is both wise and necessary to spend the time and effort to learn about the cultural environment you are entering. Follow the wisdom of the multinational giants of business and learn about Mexico's culture and people.

Often U.S. and Canadian businesspersons are described as being set in their ways. When inelastic traders venture into Mexico, where flexibility is all important, they encounter roadblocks often of their own making. Frustration, disappointment, and discouragement follow. Cultural sensitivity can eliminate most of these stumbling blocks and open many new paths to profit.

Nowhere in the world will you find two countries sharing a huge common border more culturally different than the United States and Mexico. Our sociological roots, ideals, and value systems differ significantly from those of Mexico's. The protectionist curtain drawn along the border for so long has been largely responsible for our differing development. The removal of this barrier presents the challenge to integrate our cultures, each country to be enriched by the input of the other. The now-thriving business between our countries has proved to be a wonderful vehicle for intercultural enrichment.

This chapter covers the basics of Mexican culture so you can be better equipped to handle the "people" part of commerce, the most important part. The rest you will learn by experience.

First we look at history; attitudes developed over more than 2000 years should not be ignored. Next, we discuss the uniquely Mexican mañana syndrome and show how you can use it to improve your business. The chapter also covers familia (family) and how its meaning in Mexico differs greatly from ours in the United States. You will learn about fiesta, women in business, and the language factor. We study what the Mexicans think of us and what we think of them. Finally, we suggest how to govern your conduct when you go to Mexico.

HISTORY OF THE PEOPLE

To conduct business successfully in Mexico, you must understand its people and their long and fascinating history. As you study the history of Mexico, remember to look at it in context. The United States is just a newcomer as a country when compared with Mexico's many thousand years of cultural development.

Space limitations prevent us from any in-depth study of Mexican history, so we recommend that you read books specifically dealing with the history of Mexico, such as Alan Riding, *Distant Neighbors*; Frank Brandenburg, *The Making of Modern Mexico*; and T. R. Fehrenback, *Fire and Blood: A History of Mexico*. You will attain a comprehension of a nation many consider mystifying and elusive.

Early Times

The known history of Mexico dates back thousands of years. The Olmecs created the first important civilization of Mexico about 1200 B.C. These people, who thrived for almost 700 years before their population of about 350,000 disappeared, were a powerful influence on the Mayan Indians.

The Maya began about 1500 B.C. and still thrive on

the Yucatan Peninsula. The first Mayan city emerged around A.D. 150. By 1200, the Maya had dispersed into several different tribes living in different areas of Mexico.

To the West, around Oaxaca, the Zapotec Indians appeared about 300 B.C. This tribe too has survived. At the same time the Toltecs appeared; they fell victims to the Chichimecas about 1200. The Chichimecas were a warrior tribe from the mythical Aztlan who appeared at the same time the Aztecs did.

The Aztecs became the strongest and most dominant people of pre-Hispanic times. In 1502, Moctezuma II became emperor and high priest of the region; he reigned until the Spanish explorer Cortes and his army, greedy for the riches of the land, killed Moctezuma and enslaved his people. The Aztecs revolted and selected Cuauhtemoc, nephew of Moctezuma, as their new emperor. Under his leadership, an offensive was launched in 1521 against Cortes and his army but failed. Cuauhtemoc was captured, and the Aztec empire died.

New Spain

With Cortes as its leader, Mexico became known as New Spain. Eventually Cortes was deposed by Spain because of his cruelty to the Indians, but the Indians were still slaves of the Spanish. Spanish rule and Mexican labor created the Mexican colonial style of architecture and furnishings, prominent in the churches and temples that have survived throughout Mexico. In 1542, the priest, Bartolomé de Las Casas freed the Indians from slavery, but Indians were still considered of a lower class and not treated with respect.

Attempt at Independence

In 1845, Texas was admitted into the Union, and Congress began looking west. In 1846, Zachary Taylor and his army occupied Los Angeles and Santa Fe and defeated Santa Anna and his army in 1847. General Winfield Scott took Mexico City and flew the American flag over the National Palace. After a last-ditch effort to save their country, young cadets wrapped themselves in the Mexican flag and jumped from Chapultepec Castle to their death rather than surrender. The cadets are known as Los Niños Heroes (The Child Heroes) and are a symbol of great pride.

In 1848, the Treaty of Guadalupe Hidalgo was signed. In exchange for $15 million, California, Texas, New Mexico, and Arizona became a part of the United States and American troops withdrew from Mexico, leaving behind a crippled country.

As Mexico began rebuilding its strength, two parties, the conservatives and the liberals, formed a government. Power was once again given to Santa Anna, and he persecuted the liberals. But he was overthrown for this behavior; Ignacio Comonfort became president in 1857 and named Benito Juárez (an Indian from Oaxaca) his vice president. Comonfort was forced to repeal the 1857 constitution and imprison Juárez; Comonfort went into exile and freed Juárez before leaving the county.

In 1861, the conservatives appealed to Europe for help, and Britain, Spain, and France came to Mexico. Britain and Spain left after being paid outstanding debts, but France occupied Mexico City in 1862 and instituted an assembly that gave power to Maximilian of Hapsburg. Maximilian and his wife Archduchess Carlotta became emperor and empress of Mexico. The United States sided with the liberals of Mexico, and liberal forces under Juárez' leadership forced Napoleon to withdraw. Maximilian was captured and executed in 1867.

Juárez returned to the presidency, but because of the turmoil of the past few years, Mexico was near bankruptcy. Juárez died of a heart attack in 1872; his vice president, Sebastian Lerdo de Tefada, assumed office, remaining president until General Porfirio Díaz led a successful armed revolt for the presidency. He was forced to step down in 1880. Manuel Gonzalez then became president and led the country for four destructive years. In 1884, Díaz again became president and won every election thereafter until 1910, when the revolution broke out.

Revolution

Under Díaz' leadership, Mexico advanced financially. He built up technology, railroads, the mining industry, and foreign investment—the country was booming. The problem was that out of almost 13 million citizens, about 3000 families virtually owned Mexico. The Indians were treated poorly and often not paid for their hard work. These conditions led to the revolution, which ousted Díaz and inducted Francisco I. Madero as Mexico's new president.

Emiliano Zapata led the support of Madero and began seizing land from the rich and returning it to the citizens of the villages. Relations between Madero and Zapata deteriorated. Madero and Zapata reached a truce that lasted only a few months. In 1911, Madero hired General Victoriano Huerta to deal with Zapata. Zapata and his people called for a new revolution. In 1912,

Pascual Orozco led a revolt in Northern Mexico but was stopped by Huerta. Later that year, Felix Díaz, General Díaz' nephew, marshaled a new rebellion; he and his forces were captured and jailed. They were freed in February 1913 by followers who advanced on the National Palace. After 10 days of fighting, the U.S. ambassador, Henry Lane Wilson, formed a pact that brought Díaz and Huerta together. Huerta then overthrew Madero and his vice president, Jose Maria Pino Suarez; they were murdered. Huerta became president.

Huerta's rule was short. Díaz' army now turned against Huerta, who was ousted from his dictatorial office and sent into exile. The second revolution had been won.

Francisco (Pancho) Villa then named General Eulalio Gutiérrez president. The brief regime was a disaster; General Gutiérrez fled. In 1915, General Alvaro Obregón retook the capital and chased out Pancho Villa. Villa fled north, raided the United States and killed 16 Americans in Columbus, New Mexico in 1916. The United States sent 10,000 troops into Mexico to find Pancho Villa. After 11 months they still had not captured him, making Pancho Villa a national hero. Pancho Villa was assassinated in 1923. Through all this, Zapata was causing trouble for the Mexican government and ravaging the country. In 1919 he was shot down by the revolutionary army of Venustiano Carranza.

Mexico Drifts

Under Carranza's leadership Mexico drifted. After leading a failed attempt on a mission in Sonora, he panicked and fled the country. His body was found riddled with bullets, and in 1920 he was declared an apparent suicide. Obregón became the new president of Mexico.

The dictator Obregón bribed his way into the good graces of the United States and pacified the country after the revolution. In 1925, he was succeeded by Plutarco Elias Calles, who tamed the political forces and built on Obregón's accomplishments. He violently eliminated his enemy and rewarded loyalties with payoffs. He founded the Bank of Mexico, instituted the first income tax, and spent heavily on education. Calles was especially hard on the Cathlic church. In 1926, Calles ordered all native-born priests to be licensed. The Catholics boycotted the churches, and peasants led by priests murdered and sab-otaged in the name of Christ. The government perse-cuted this militant group, known as the Cristeros. Priests were hung, and Cristeros were massacred. The dispute ended in 1929, but looting and face-offs continued.

Calles' four-year term was ending. He amended the constitution, enabling Obregón to run again. He ex-tended the presidential term from four to six years. Those who rebelled were executed. Obregón was re-elected but days later assassinated by Jose de Leon Toral, a newspaper cartoonist and devout Catholic. Calles once again became leader of the nation.

Birth of PNR

Upon his departure from office in 1929, Calles organized the strong and powerful National Revolutionary Party (PNR). The PNR appeared in the 1929 election. Emilio Portes Gil, a lawyer, had been named and served as pres-ident until the 1929 election. In 1932, Calles named General Abelardo Rodriguez president of Mexico. A new election was held in 1934; General Lázaro Cárdenas was elected Mexico's new president. Cárdenas was popular and considered a president of the people. He formed the National Peasant Confederation (CNC), the Confederation of Mexican Workers (CTM), and the Worker and Peasant Confederation for Mexico (CGOCM). He nationalized foreign railroad companies in 1937, handing over management to the railroad workers. His most monumental act was nationalizing the oil companies in 1937. A slump in the economy, a devaluation of currency, a freeze on investments, and a wave of inflation followed, along with complicated world relations. Mexico was saved from collapse by World War II.

With Cárdenas' continuing popularity, more organizations were formed. In 1940, Cárdenas handed over his post to Manuel Avila Camacho, the defense minister, and Mexico had a new president. During Camacho's regime and World War II, Mexico's industrial revolution began. The United States bought raw materials from Mexico. Local manufacturing was on the upswing. Thousands of Mexicans were employed in both Mexico and the United States. Inflation, corruption, and lack of price and quality control rose sharply as Mexico became industrialized.

In 1946, Miguel Alemán was nominated president of Mexico and became Camacho's successor. He renamed the PNR the Institutional Revolutionary Party (PRI). Under Alemán's leadership, massive industrialization, urbanization, economic growth, emergence of a big-spending middle class, and neglect of social problems occurred. Younger leaders assumed power, and the Mexican government became a bureaucracy. Alemán believed in growth first, justice later. The country grew, and so did its corruption as the Mexican officals became very rich. In 1952, Adolfo Ruiz Cortines was chosen Alemán's successor; he gave women the right to vote. Cortines was succeeded by Adolfo López Mateos in 1958.

The young Mateos brought changes to Mexico. He gave land to the peasants, built up the education system, expanded the social security system, and traveled extensively abroad. In 1964 he was succeeded by Gustavo Díaz Ordaz.

The 1968 Olympic Games

The 1968 Olympics were held in Mexico during Ordaz' term, angering many people in Mexico who believed that the money should have been spent on more pressing matters. Protests erupted throughout the country, and massacres, arrests, and general oppression reigned. The games continued, but what the cameras did not show were the thousands of armed soldiers surrounding the Aztec Stadium.

In 1969, Luis Echeverria Alvarez became president of Mexico. He released the political prisoners of 1968 and opened communications between Mexico and the rest of the world. Private investment slowed, and the government began borrowing money. The currency was devalued once again, and corruption increased. To everyone's surprise, Alvarez chose as his successor Jose Lopez Portillo, a man who had almost no political experience and little interest in government.

From Boom to Bust

Under Portillo, Mexico boomed. Spending increased, profits rose, oil finds were large and numerous, the peso stabilized, and the private sector enjoyed its wealth. On the down side, inflation increased, spending exceeded oil revenues, and growth rose. The world wanted Mexico's oil, and countries were begging to lend Mexico money.

In 1981, world oil prices dropped. Mexico then began borrowing heavily. In 1982, the peso was devalued yet again, and banks were nationalized. Mexico was in crisis. Portillo was known as Mexico's devalued president and left office a beaten man. His successor was the Harvard-educated Miguel de la Madrid, who had a strong background in economics. Holding office during the worst of times, his goals were to stop corruption and make Mexico more efficient. He lowered spending and living standards, controlled imports, and raised prices. Industrial production and Mexico's purchasing power were both on a downswing. Madrid did what he could to bandage the wounds during his six-year term.

The Modern Era Emerges

President Carlos Salinas de Gortari is credited with bringing Mexico into the modern era. His administration attacked all of Mexico's woes at once. Mexico was struggling to service its burdensome debt. The U.S. Brady plan provided for partial forgiveness of debt and a restructuring of the payment schedule to give Mexico a chance to get on its feet.

The Salinas administration then coordinated the largest series of privatizations of state-owned industries in history. Some 1000 state institutions were returned to private hands, and literally billions of dollars were raised. More investment money entered the country as the economic reform movement gathered momentum and looked to be successful.

Capitalizing on this momentum and using public

relations to the maximum, Salinas succeeded in bringing back billions in flight capital, lowering inflation
from 180 percent to less than 20 percent, using government and business to rebuild Mexico's physical and economic infrastructure, and much more.

THE MAÑANA SYNDROME

The mañana syndrome is basic to Mexican business. Understand what it is, how it works, and how to use it in
your favor and you will prosper in business. But deny
the mañana syndrome or try to change this engrained
cultural phenomenon and you will fail.

The word "mañana" is translated literally as "tomorrow." But figuratively, the word has a different
meaning. The naive U.S. businessperson uses mañana
derogatorily, suggesting that Mexicans procrastinate.
But what at first seems to be procrastination is merely
the different way Mexican businesspeople prioritize their
lives and activities. When doing business in Mexico, you
need to know when to kick butt and when to kick back.
Know where the dividing line is between these two concepts and you will control the mañana syndrome.

The Mexican businessperson's system of priorities
is family and social obligations first and business later.
A seeming indifference to your immediate problems or
opportunity is merely the Mexican's dignity and "cool"
under pressure. The Mexican business environment is
more easygoing than that in the overly aggressive,
stressed-out United States, but easygoing charm is *not*
the same as laziness. The energetic and industrious Mexicans deal with things one step at a time.

Initially you will be shocked at the two- to four-hour daily lunches. Everyone from the marketplace vendor to the top-level executive follows this daily ritual. So do not even think of calling a Mexican business between the hours of 2:00 and 4:00 because no one is there. Whereas the United States businessperson does a networking-power-brainstorming lunch of sprouts and decaf, with agendas, microcassettes, and audiovisuals, the Mexican is enjoying a colorful and relaxed multicourse meal. Conversation rarely touches on the specifics of business; talk of family and friends is the rule.

It is absolutely wrong for the visiting United States businessperson to try to overcome the Mexican "We'll attend to this later" luncheon attitude, which is all part of their concept of mañana. Regardless of how hurried, harried, or hassled you may be, do *not* show it. In a country where business is done only with "friends," the ritual business lunch is an opportunity for the Mexicans to take your measure, judging you by your cool and by your attention to family and social concerns. Thus, this indeed is a business lunch. Your response to the mañana attitude tells the Mexicans about you as a person and enables them to decide whether you will be an asset to their business or an unnecessary annoyance.

There is plenty of time for business. After lunch, most people work until 7:00 or later in the evening. Different culture, different hours, and different priorities perhaps leads to greater productivity. When the Mexican gets down to business, you will be surprised at the speed and efficiency used to get the job done. Without apparent effort, astounding results are forthcoming.

Now for the important message. You can see that to be accepted in Mexican business, you must embrace the relaxed way of doing business. At no point, however, consider becoming less vigilant. In Mexico, as everywhere, there are lazy and work-shy people. You must deal with them expeditiously, just as you would in the United States.

The mañana syndrome also directly affects the setting of deadlines. "Deadline" has a somewhat different meaning in Mexico. Every contract in Mexico has an implied granting of an extension for important events. So in determining deadlines, you must factor in the Mexican businessperson's sense of priorities and urgency. Schedule your deadlines to be flexible. For example, if you absolutely need something done by May 1, give an April 10 deadline; you will have your results on time. Furthermore, consider that a two-week contract around Easter means four weeks. To illustrate, in week 1, work begins. In week 2, a little work gets done, but the main emphasis is on getting ready for Easter week. In week 3, Easter week, nothing gets done in Mexican business. In week 4, work starts slowly but is done by the weekend.

Business in Mexico is a matter of understanding parameters and working within them. Once you adjust to the favorable concept of mañana, you will find this a pleasing and exciting challenge. Learning to distinguish between incompetence and cool is the heart of using the mañana syndrome to your advantage. Initially you may need guidance from someone more experienced, but you will quickly catch on and learn while enjoying some fine company and dining.

IMPORTANCE OF FAMILY

Family is the glue that holds together the fabric of Mexican society during periods of rebellion, economic devastation, and persecution. Understanding this ethic is critical to your success in Mexico's business circles. Nothing is more sacred to a Mexican than family; it is the foundation on which Mexican life is built.

The Mexican concept of familia means so much more than its literal translation of "family." In the United States, cousins can go entire lifetimes without meeting, brothers without speaking; children move great distances and lose contact; family reunions are rare; and divorce is rampant. But for the Mexican, family is the main source of joy and pride. A Mexican family frequently includes five generations. The women marry quite young (by U.S. standards) and continue producing children even after having grandchildren. Thus, at a Mexican family gathering (often each Sunday), the generations become blurred, perhaps explaining the lack of a generation gap.

The man is the undisputed head of the family. The woman is the mother, above all else, and revered as such. Mexican social life commonly centers around family get-togethers, and marriages are often alliances between families. Elders are honored rather than ridiculed and forgotten. Children are taught to respect adults, and in return, adults seem to respect children.

Holidays, of which there are many in Mexico, are when the extended family shines. For peasant and politico both, holidays are a family event, the likes of which are rarely seen in the United States. The teenagers do not look bored; they are where they want to be and are wanted. They are proud of their family and know their heritage.

When invited into a Mexican home, look into the people's eyes. They are excited that you are meeting the family. They welcome you and the opportunity to show their success. This is it, and they are proud of it. It is a great honor to be welcomed into the usually closed

confines of the Mexican family home, and you must rec-
ognize it as such. The family is on display for you, so
you should acknowledge the household and its pride.

In business, do not expect the Mexican to shove
aside family concerns until the end of the deal. It will not
happen, and it is insulting to even raise such an issue.
Honor the Mexican family and you will gain respect.
Remember, this is more than just grandparents exchang-
ing baby pictures. This is their history, their culture,
their life, and their pride.

CELEBRATIONS WITH THE DEAD

Mysticism is as much a part of Mexican cultural development as patriotism and pride. From the Aztec gods
and the Mayan idols to the modern day Dia del Muerto
(Day of the Dead), this mystical side of Mexican society
should be acknowledged and understood, to give you a
little more insight into the Mexican as a whole person,
not simply a business associate.

November 2 is the Dia del Muerto. Although not an
official holiday, its celebration is widespread. It is a time
of communion with one's ancestors in a down-to-earth
Mexican way. Families crowd the cemeteries, bringing
huge feasts. Loved ones gather on and around the graves
of their departed relatives. Dining is picnic style as children frolic throughout the grounds and have a great
time. Squealing youngsters bat piñatas decorated as ske-
letons until they give up their hidden treasures of candy
and treats.

These celebrations not only honor the ancestors,
they also mock death, almost as the Aztecs did. Families

are reunited with the spirits of their forefathers and cele-
brate with them. Memories, as well as history, are an
important source of pride to the Mexican.

PLEASURE ABOVE ALL ELSE

Why do Mexican workers seem happier than their U.S.
counterparts? How can they work those incredible
hours? Why would the concept of "stress management
workshops" be laughable in Mexico? Mexicans understand the concept of fiesta, an important part of the Mexican spirit. If you understand fiesta and factor it into
your business plans, you will prosper.

Despite countless instances of betrayal, tragedy,
plunder, and defeat in Mexico's history, the Mexican
society is not bitter and cynical; Mexicans are a charm-
ing people with a smile in their hearts. Perhaps more
than any other nationality, the Mexicans believe that life
is for enjoyment. This zest for life is pervasive in all
segments of their population. Pleasure for its own sake
is what the Mexicans seek. It is their reward for their
labors and never far from their minds.

The notion of fiesta as we use it in this book does
not suggest idleness in the workplace. Fiesta is what car-
ries the Mexicans through arduous tasks—they know
fun is on the way. They do not wait for their two weeks
a year as we do in the United States. Celebrations are
frequent and joyous.

On a recent trip to Mexico we were introducing a
client to the fascinating and beautiful city of Cuernavaca. After a visit to Cortes' summer palace and a trip to
the zocalo (town square), we stopped in front of an office

building under construction. Our associate was amazed to see workers climbing rickety scaffolding carrying 100-pound stones to be hand-placed into the walls. Such exhaustive labor would dampen any but the Mexican spirit. Here there were laughter and teasing as even the frailest workers carried their weight in stone. We soon learned the reason for this levity. Some 20 minutes later, as we were dining on the grounds of Las Mañanitas (one of Mexico's premier hostelries known only to insiders), we heard gunfire coming from the direction of the construction site. The gracious proprietor instantly appeared at our table to calm our concerns. Noontime began Mexico's version of our Labor Day, a time of fiesta for all Mexican workers and their families.

A Mexican fiesta is always gay and colorful. It can take place anywhere and at any time. Without hesitation, a Mexican worker will spend an entire week's earnings to show friends a good time. Free-flowing tequila, colorful piñatas for the children, vibrantly dressed señoritas, manly señores, and the ever-present mariachi bands appear out of nowhere. The fiesta is on! Sunrise brings another workday, and the workers are back with a glint in their eye. Work-related stress appears nonexistent.

In Mexico's work force, foreign companies are finding higher productivity, less frequent illness, and fewer injuries than in the United States. The work force is also quite stable. A big factor is the fiesta attitude of pleasure above all else.

WOMEN IN BUSINESS

At every conference we attend and at each class we teach, particularly in the field of corporate employee relocation

training, we are asked about women in Mexico's business community. Will Mexican businessmen take a
woman seriously? Will they be condescending toward
her? American women fear that business opportunity in
Mexico is closed to them and worry that their time, effort, and money will be wasted. But nothing is further
from the truth, although it is true that Mexico's business
community is very male dominated, with historically
sexist attitudes.

Here is your edge in Mexico if you are a woman.
The men who run the businesses and government are
gentlemen in the classic sense. They will be polite and
take your call or assist in any way possible. Doing so
might be annoying to them, but you will always get an
audience. Respect is the key to business in Mexico, and
women have the advantage of starting out "respected."
But do not misunderstand and think that you have a
full-time advantage. You have only a leg up (pardon the
expression) on your male competition; all you get is an
audience, and you get it quickly.

Once in your meeting, you will be expected to be
competent and have a profitable business proposition.
The Mexicans running the country and business are not
stupid. You got your hearing; now it is up to your talent
alone to outdistance your male competition.

Mexican businesswomen are sharp. They did not get
to their positions of power by flirting; they worked for
it. Many Mexican businesswomen can hold their own
against the sharpest male U.S. counterparts. They dress
well, and femininely. They are gracious hostesses and
even more gracious guests. In business they never forget
that they are women, and they never let anyone else forget
it either. Thus, "successful women" in Mexican business
is not an oxymoron. If you are sharp, you will do great.

One final caveat for businesswomen headed to Mexico. Never give a Mexican businessman's wife any reason to dislike you or to be jealous. At all costs guard against awaking the jealousy of the Mexican wife. Because of the Mexican stress on the home, potential or perceived homewreckers are shown no mercy.

THE LANGUAGE FACTOR

The question we hear most often is "Do we need to speak Spanish to do business in Mexico?" No, you need not be fluent in Spanish to be successful in Mexico, but there are many compelling reasons to learn the language.

The education system in Mexico, both formal and at home, considers a second (or even third) language of utmost importance. Everyone realizes that they are global citizens and not isolated in their country. Thus, you will find that a great many people speak English, some not so well but others very fluently, so you can get by without speaking Spanish because most of the people you will be doing business will speak English. But this book is not for people who just want to get by. This book is for the businessperson who wants to enter new markets and be on the cutting edge of international opportunity. Good businesspeople realize that communication is a very important part of commerce. For increased effectiveness with customers, employees, suppliers, and shippers, you need to pay attention to communication. In Mexico, this means that you must learn some Spanish.

Being respected is of utmost importance in Mexican business. One way to begin earning this respect is to learn about Mexico's culture and language. The Mexicans study our language and culture as part of their education. And many significant business transactions will hinge on your host's perception of your long-term commitment to Mexico. That is, are you just in this for a quick profit, or is this the beginning of a long and profitable relationship? Learning the language is surely evidence of such a commitment.

How hard is learning the language? Except for just a few verbs, not as difficult as you may think. Try the many available books, tapes, and classes. As you practice and learn, step up to newspapers, magazines, and the local Spanish television station. The more you are exposed to the language, the easier it is and the faster you will learn.

Do not be shy. Try out your fledgling skills at every opportunity. The people will not laugh—they will be pleased to help refine your speech. The more you immerse yourself, the faster you will learn. Understanding the language will enhance both your business and culture experiences and open more avenues.

When it is time to negotiate business, fluency in Spanish wins you immediate respect and gives you an advantage. On the other hand, if your language skills are anything less than perfect, bring along a Spanish-speaking adviser. Because nuances are important, select your adviser carefully.

RELATIONS BETWEEN COUNTRIES

Historically, relations between Mexico and the United States have been tense. By the early nineteenth century,

Mexico perceived the United States as land grabbing, and rightly so since we stole about half their country. (Had Mexico's army been a bit more skilled, California, Texas, Arizona, and New Mexico might have remained Mexico's northernmost states.) In the United States, people believed that despots in Mexico City were trying to control open territories far distant from the capital, populated with people feeling no allegiance to the regime. This was the period of maximum division between the two countries.

The twentieth century brought with it both good and bad relations between the United States and Mexico. The Mexican government generally had a protectionist view of us, openly demonstrating a distrust of the United States and its reputation for taking land. Several Mexican presidents did seek favor with the United States, but their overtures rarely achieved much because they were motivated by either political rhetoric or personal gain. Throughout this period, the United States continued to strengthen its border and view its southern neighbor as a poor relation.

The situation changed fast when the "poor relative" discovered oil. Overnight the United States was courting its southern friend with a vengeance. New to such wealth, somewhat inflated with self-importance, and spotting the U.S. duplicity, Mexican leaders sought to rebuild from within. Trade between our countries became expensive and difficult. Relations were strained as never before.

As we discussesd earlier, the Salinas administration changed the entire picture of foreign trade and investment almost overnight. Effectively opening the borders to trade and openly inviting U.S. investment in many industries, President Salinas' group began the rebuilding of the Mexican economy. The United States was quick to respond to these new opportunities. Mexico's newly stable economy and a future of unprecedented growth gave the United States a new outlook.

Today, Mexico and the United States apparently have set aside historical differences and are discovering countless ways the businesses and governments can complement each other. We need room—they have it. We need an economical labor force to compete in the world economy—they offer it. They need foreign trade—we can provide it. They need access to capital goods and technology—we are providing them. Mexico is our neighbor, and our needs intermesh.

We are now at a unique time in history. Both the United States and Mexico have passed the testing the water stage and are wholeheartedly seeking to improve and expand relations. Business is leading the way, but confusion still prevails as our countries economically integrate. With business and industry scrambling to position themselves for the long term, a window of possible and staggering profits has appeared. This is a time of unprecedented opportunity. Relations between our countries are particularly excellent and getting better.

ATTITUDES TOWARD FOREIGNERS

The surest path to success with the people of Mexico is to grasp the essence of their attitudes toward foreigners. If you govern yourself accordingly, the path is easy, with seemingly impenetrable barriers disappearing and the impossible becoming possible. But if you fail to understand how Mexicans feel toward us or if you ignore such feelings, your venture will be doomed to mediocrity at best.

They Think We Are Fools

Let's not mince words. The Mexicans expect us to be fools, the "ugly American," loud, blustering, and arrogant. The ugly American knows three words of Spanish and looks down on Mexicans who do not understand their meaning; the ugly American substitutes volume for vocabulary and thinks any situation can be controlled by throwing money around.

They See Us As Being Wasteful

To a country where thrift is a way of life, our ostentatious displays of wealth offend. Compare the Mexican height of style—an immaculate Grand Marquis with driver—to our stretched-out "don't spare the chrome" limo. The Mexicans are happy to take our money when we throw it around, but we certainly are not buying respect.

Mexicans Question Our Society's Value System

In Mexico, the family is *everything,* no exceptions. As the Mexicans see us, we are always business, business, business, with little regard for the family. The Mexicans question a society whose measure of value depends on ability to produce income.

The Mexicans wonder if they can trust us. Without the strong foundation of a family life, what sort of values do we bring to our business ventures? Despite their image of the American people, the Mexicans' warm heart and graciousness shine through. They will give us a chance to prove ourselves. We are welcomed with open arms and treated with respect as individuals. Eliminate the flamboyance, remember your manners, and you will be treated as family.

All this closely affects how your business will fare. Our concept of networking is a sixth sense in the Mexicans. Their resourcefulness is constantly astounding. Whether you are seeking a visa exemption or the disposition of hundreds of tons of wood chips, everyone knows someone connected in some way to your requirements. Personal referral is treated with great respect in Mexico and is often the only way to get something done. Be worthy of this no-strings-attached friendship and you will thrive in Mexico, gradually building networks of your own.

The Mexicans are quite sharp at seeing people for what they are. Their attitudes toward us are based on painfully accurate observations. They are charitable enough to accept us initially, notwithstanding the buffoonery of our citizens. Prove yourself and they will help you. Ignore their initial attitudes at your peril.

NATIONAL PRIDE

Doing business successfully in Mexico requires an understanding of the many facets of the country's complex society. Pride is especially important in Mexican life: self-pride, country pride, and family pride.

You particularly feel this pride when touring any city with some local people. From the small village with a statue of a never-to-be-forgotten hero in their zocalo to the great Reforma of Mexico City, monuments are everywhere. (The Reforma is the multilane avenue running through the heart of Mexico City. It was built as an exact duplicate of the Champs Élysées in Paris.)

So evident is Mexican pride in their nation and its history that you are never out of sight of a glorietta (a large circle of ground in the center of the street around which traffic flows). In the glorietta's center there is always a grand monument to Mexican history. All natives are unofficial tour guides as they point out the monuments and commemorations, telling you their significance in Mexican history. They beam with pride as you are swept up in the spirit and seek out yet more markers and monuments to the great events and heroes of Mexico. Picture a Fourth of July celebration in a small U.S. town. The overt manifestation of pride in our nation is what Mexico is like year-round. Their party decorations are in the national colors, and a flag is in every home.

Nowhere can you feel the Mexicans' sense of nation more than in the arts. Their music, productions, paintings, and song all glorify some moment of history or culture. The National Folkloric Ballet is always a sellout. There are always more locals than tourists, and you are treated to two hours of Star Spangled Banner–type chills. Mexican national pride is contagious and should be an important consideration in your business plans and negotiations. (Later we discuss how to respond to every businessperson's first question: "How long have you been here and what have you done?")

It is certainly a benefit to business and a boost to trade that Mexico is so secure with its national identity. Many of the original Canadian concerns about open trade, including fear of being absorbed by the U.S. economy if free trade proceeded, do not apply to Mexico. The poor villagers who trek many miles to a civic parade, the citizens who watch the unveiling of a new monument to Mexico's leaders—all Mexicans know that their country is number one in the world. Throughout history, their countless heroes have shown that no sacrifice is too great for Mexico.

AMERICAN RULES DO NOT APPLY

In the 1960s, President John Kennedy went to Germany. Through an interpreter he gave an emotional speech to the assembled crowd. At the end the audience went wild as he spoke the German words "Ich bin ein Berliner." Here in the United States we were warmed by the cheering multitudes, touched that he had learned a local expression. We later learned that the spectators were laughing because our well-meaning president had declared with a passion, "I am a doughnut." The point is, when you are out of the United States, you must be particularly sensitive to cultural differences to avoid embarrassment and problems. Dan Quayle certainly lost respect when proclaiming that he hoped he remembered his high school Latin during his stay in Latin America!

Foolish blunders are not limited to the political arena. U.S. businesses have followed some disastrous marketing strategies as they entered the Mexican market. General Motors is a huge company with a reputation for business acumen. You'd think they would retain bicultural marketing specialists before entering this new market. But they spent a fortune on a slickly presented advertising campaign introducing the Chevy Nova to Mexico. Nobody wanted one. Why? "No va," translated directly, means "Doesn't go."

Other U.S. companies have lost fortunes by not using culturally aware marketing talent. A major clothing company almost failed after adopting a slogan that when translated into Spanish means "Until I put on this shirt I felt great." McDonald's franchises were actually closed for a short time while government officials explained Mexico's disliking the use of their flag on McDonald's promotional napkins.

The Matador, a sexy and macho name for a car in the United States, did not make it in Mexico because "matador" means "killer." Once again we find that American rules do not apply. (We will not trouble you with the car named "ugly old woman.") Consider Braniff, which wanted a share of the lucrative Mexican market. All of Mexico was brought to their knees with laughter as Braniff's multimillion-dollar ad campaign hit the streets. When translated, their "Fly in Leather" commercials suggested flying "naked." "Where are you going?" "I'm going to Acapulco, and I'm flying naked." Where is Braniff these days anyway?

Coors and Budweiser were the beer industry's embarrassments. "Turn it loose" translated into "Suffer from diarrhea," and "King of beers" translated to "Queen of beers." And every Mexican remembers the U.S. chicken company with the slogan "It takes a tough man to make a tender chicken"; the message conveyed to the Mexicans came out as "It takes a sexually stimulated man to make a chicken affectionate."

If you are in business for yourself or represent a U.S. company, you know the primary reason for your success. You understand the people you serve, their wants, needs, and motivations. But as you can see from the above disasters, what works in the United States does not necessarily work well in Mexico. A small blunder or social faux pas can seriously damage business. Woe to the pushy businessperson who offends a Customs Official.

In the United States, pushy sometimes works. Occasionally the John Wayne approach of clearing obstacles with guns blazing is well received. Mexicans, on the other hand, believe that "quiet is cool." The subtleties of an Al Pacino or Robert De Niro approach will get you much further than loud macho aggressiveness.

Respect is the order of the day in Mexican life and business. You earn respect by taking the time to learn the customs and cultural differences. In Chapter 10 you will learn about business etiquette, relationships, the necessity for patience, and social adeptness in Mexico. The lesson of this section is that American rules do not apply in Mexico. You must know the differences for your business venture to begin well. Failing to understand or acknowledge them can cause your company great harm, if not doom it to failure.

3

Entrepreneur's Promised Land

New Markets

Every U.S. entrepreneur occasionally thinks back to the period between 1929 and 1932: "What I could have done with just a little capital!" Those few people with capital and vision at that dark time in our nation's history built the beginnings of empires and shaped the future of our country. At the end of the Depression, those people were firmly established, and they prospered as new markets with eager consumers came through the floodgates. A similar boom occurred after World War II. The onset of peace released a consumer demand that the informed had anticipated, resulting in new markets and huge profits during a period of unprecedented growth.

Now we are in the 1990s. We are being told to accept less as being OK. Consumer confidence is down, and the economy is debt-ridden. Companies that grew huge over the decades now control entire markets. There is little room for newcomers, and profit margins are slim. Super-markets carry at least 65 brands of cereal, all provided by just a few companies. Established companies rule the competition because shaky banks will not lend to start-ups, and private capital is scarce. Our rate of savings is absurdly low.

The true entrepreneur now faces the choices of scratching and begging for a tiny piece of the pie, eking out a miserable existence, or going for the gold. Gold to-day means new products, new markets, new partnerships, new opportunities—all available in Mexico. Mexico has been miraculously emerging from economic Dark Ages. Private industry is struggling to meet new demands, and the international trade scale is reaching new peaks. More than 100 million Mexican consumers want and need more goods and services after going without for so long. Pre-viously existing businesses cannot adequately serve this large consumer base. Efficient distribution, production, and marketing are only now appearing. Formerly state-owned and state-run businesses are being privatized, so they must become efficient, profitable, and competitive.

There are new markets for profit, assuredly. Capital goods are scarce and in demand. From agriculture to tourism, publishing to mining, the new less restrictive environment for foreigners (us) coupled with a growth economy make the serving of Mexican markets a tre-mendous opportunity. Remember 1929. Think of 100 million Mexican consumers. Consider an entire country rebuilding its infrastructure. Take advantage of the op-portunities. If you have the vision to see the needs of Mexico, the flexibility to adapt to a different environ-ment, and the speed to take advantage of this tremendous window of opportunity, you can find your place in this promised land.

ROOM TO GROW

Mexico is huge, and its terrain varied. You need a sense of geography as a frame of reference as we discuss regional business opportunities. The country is shaped like a cornucopia, the symbol of abundance. If geography can be considered prophetic, surely Mexico is a country overflowing with opportunity.

The Mexican land mass covers 760,000 square miles, with thousands of miles of coastlines, jungles, forest lands, soaring mountains, deserts, and farmlands. Mexico's northern border is the United States' southern border. To the east is the Yucatan Peninsula, with its shores in the Gulf of Mexico and the Caribbean. To the west is the Baja Peninsula, separated from Mexico's mainland by the Sea of Cortez.

There is tremendous geographical diversity in Mexico. Mexico City, the center of government and industry, has a population of 20 million people. At the other end of the spectrum are the peaceful villages of Oaxaca. Each area of Mexico has its own distinct personality, each region its customs and sports teams. Each state's development is directly affected by its geography. The country is divided into 31 states and the federal district of Mexico City, much like the United States and Washington, DC.

For all its beauty and diversity, Mexico does have some problems the government is working at solving, and in so doing is creating opportunities for business. Mexico City, Guadalajara, Monterrey, and certain border areas have a disproportionate share of Mexico's business and industry. The areas are dangerously overpopulated as industry grows and more people crowd the cities for employment. The result is serious pollution, crowding, congestion, crime, and more.

Another problem is traffic. The Los Angeles freeways are like country roads compared to some memorable Reforma jams. But Mexicans do have a good attitude about traffic. We were at the height of gridlock one afternoon—the army actually had to come in to untangle the five-mile back up—when everyone gave up, turned off their cars, and staged an impromptu fiesta. We all had a great time and met new friends in a stress-free environment while awaiting the army's help.

Despite the problems in these areas, Mexico has open and airy areas. Labor is plentiful and less expensive, and the cost of living is significantly less in the country than in the city. Beautiful, untouched areas are ready for tourism, and huge, open areas await manufacturing facilities. And the government is ready to help you!

If you are in a business that the government is promoting, such as tourism (yes, you can now effectively own coastal property), and meet size and financing requirements, the government will provide great incentives. If you want to manufacture in an area not already overdeveloped, you will receive tremendous advantages.

Besides government support, other factors encourage our investment. A business needs room to grow. Instead of engaging in detailed negotiations over a 10-year lease with options and escalations on a small spot in Mexico City, you can buy and develop or hold land across the street from your plant outside the cities. You can build as the need arises and actually own, instead of being tied to an inflexible lease on scarce space. Mexico is almost a businessperson's heaven. You can conduct business in a place with few boundaries and lots of room for growth. Make inquiries in the areas that might suit your needs. What sounds better: another motel in Marina Del Rey, or an ocean-front resort in just about to boom Huatulco? Doing some homework will definitely prove worthwhile.

NATURAL RESOURCES

Mexico is a country with abundant natural resources. Its economy, politics, and world position have changed dramatically over the past 15 years by one resource alone: oil. In a rags to riches to rags to stability story, Mexico's recent history has been tied to the discovery, management, and reliance on this important resource. The country's future is more diverse. The planned uses of the other abundant resources will take Mexico into the next century.

Oil has been Mexico's most important natural resource. But suddenly becoming a world leader in oil exports led to misjudgments by Mexico's leaders, for which the country paid dearly. When oil prices were at their height, Mexico and its politicians were suddenly in the world's spotlight, courted by bankers with endless supplies of available loans. This newfound wealth enabled Mexico's decision makers to put other economic concerns on the back burner by handling problems with oil money or oil loan funds. But then oil prices crashed, and with them the rest of Mexico's mismanaged economy. Only now is Mexico seeing the light of economic recovery after 12 years of struggling back. Oil is still important, providing much needed revenues from the world market. Lessons have been learned, however, and Mexico is now diversifying through use of its many other natural resources. It has a great deal of oil but is no longer using it as a crutch. Foreign capital and technology are being sought to help develop the country.

Mining resources include silver, copper, lead, and zinc. Mexico is the world's largest producer of silver, and just one copper mine supplies three percent of the world's supply. Mexico has tremendous amounts of raw materials, and further development of these resources will create major opportunities throughout the 1990s.

Agriculture too is important in Mexico, but only now are restrictions being eased so that the most can be made of Mexico's best farming areas. As technology and fewer restrictions increase the productivity of usable agricultural land, room for growth also increases.

Mexico has limited forests and is trying to use them to their best advantage. Most wood products must be imported, but the timber industry is still young in the Copper Mountain and other areas. Ecological concerns will limit, we hope, the rate of development in this area.

North America's favorite sportfishing areas are also the home of Mexico's commercial fishing industry. Commercial fishing was formerly restricted to Mexican nationals on a "strategic resource" basis but now is open to limited outside investment and remains one of Mexico's important resources.

Mexico's abundance of resources is a solid basis for its economic growth and diversification. These raw resources will fuel economic development, and domestic production for export will provide additional growth and stability. Rather than fighting for scarce U.S. resources or relying on imported goods, wouldn't it be wiser to look to Mexico? Economic and resource integration between our countries is growing. Consider how you might join the prosperity.

PRIVATIZATION

If you asked 100 U.S. businesspeople to list the factors that would create an ideal business environment, they would all agree on at least one thing: business should run business, and government should tend to governing. During Mexico's protectionist years, many industries were nationalized, that is, removed from private ownership and made state owned and operated. Administration policies felt that industries such as banking, petroleum, and communications were giving foreigners too much control of Mexico's economy. Suddenly Mexico's government was in the business community in a big way. With vast amounts of oil revenue pouring in and no outside competition for the major industries, businesses became overstaffed and inefficient. But that just did not matter because there was enough money from the oil to fix any apparent problem. Add to this no-motivation-for-productivity environment significant corruption, and you can imagine what happened.

Oil revenues crashed and the scope of the disaster became evident. No more money was available to disguise the inefficiencies. What was left was an almost irredeemable quagmire of business wreckage. Mexico's business infrastructure was in a shambles. Under the administration of President De La Madrid, foundations to save the situation were laid, but he and his group were too busy bandaging the economy to really get ahead. The credit for taking the bull by the horns and making sweeping changes in government ownership of business goes to the Salinas administration. With exceptional talent, showmanship, charisma, timing, marketing, and not just a little bluff, the administration orchestrated the most incredible privatization program in history. Here we look at some of the results; individual industry overviews are further discussed in the following chapter, including specific opportunities available now that the privatization program is in full force. The telephone, banking, oil, transportation, and agriculture industries have been or are being returned to private ownership and control.

Phone System

Mexico's state-run and state-owned telephone system was recently privatized in one of the largest and most successful stock offerings in the history of communications. The country needs a modern communication system if it is to have any hope of improving its standing in the world business community. When Telmex was privatized, the communications infrastructure was in a shambles. There had been no new capital for capital improvements, and any repairs had been shoddy and infrequent. Now, in a bold program of modernization, rebuilding, and expansion, billions of dollars are being spent annually and will continue to be for the foreseeable future. Satellites, fiber optics, cellular advances, and other futuristic communications hardware are now, for Mexico, things of the present and the very near future. The stock is doing great, service is better, foreign companies are getting contracts, and Mexico's communications future looks secure. Privatization has worked wonders.

Banks

Inefficiencies, a worsening economy, bad loans, and even corruption were sending Mexico's banks down the drain.

Once again, brilliant marketing and timing of sales are raising totally unforeseeable amounts of cash. With billions of dollars from the sale of large banks and millions of dollars coming in from the sales of smaller banks, the government is declaring bank privatization a success.

As with communications, banks are racing to modernize with new computer networks, ATMs, new deposits, new services, and much more. Mexico's banking system is now in the hands of business, and it is thriving. New deposits from increased foreign trade and investment, some return of flight capital, and new profits from new efficiencies have Mexico's banks on a stable course. Conversely, the vast amount of capital raised from the sales is providing the government with resources to promote more trade and investment. All this helps the banks and other industries. The momentum is building as Mexico's economy is rebuilding at an incredible pace.

Oil and Petrochemicals

Oil is Mexico's most dollar valuable asset at this time. Any possible privatization of Pemex (Mexico's state-owned oil monopoly) is a very politically sensitive issue, the concern being that if the country's most valuable resource is controlled by non-Mexicans, then foreigners would control the future of the Mexican people.

In what might be called a continuous "semiprivatization," portions of the oil industry are now being run by the business community. The government sees this action as necessary because infrastructure improvement is absolutely necessary to maintain this precious resource, and research and development have been at a standstill since the crash of oil prices in the early 1980s.

Under this semiprivatization, the government has reduced by literally hundreds of items the list of petrochemical products restricted to the government. Furthermore, gas station franchises are the latest thing. Also, foreign companies have been receiving exploration contracts on a joint venture basis. Look for this trend of oil privatization, a little at a time, to continue. As Mexico modernizes and its population increases, there will be an increasing demand for oil and its products locally. Just to keep up, vast infrastructure improvements must be made, and this takes capital. Also, if domestic demand eats up all the oil, Mexico will lose its oil-export capability, an incredibly important source of foreign capital.

Transportation

Transportation encompasses roads, rail, air, ports, shipping, and more. This category includes everything from the full-blown privatization of the airlines to the "only for a couple of years" privatization for some roads and highways. Ports are somewhere in between, and the railroads will have to soon follow. As with communications and banking, a modern system of transportation will also be necessary for Mexico to accomplish its "First World" goals. Products and people need freedom of movement for a country to work efficiently.

The roads are horrible in many parts of the country. Short-term repairs were the rule during the protectionist period, and now the wear is more than just showing. Rebuilding the roads of an entire nation is a tall order, but a journey of 1000 miles begins with just one step. Mexico's first step is to allow private companies to build a number of important roads; these roads will soon be toll roads, with the tolls used to recover the cost of building and return a profit to the builders. Then the privatization, in theory, will be over, and the roads will be returned to the government. This undertaking is fairly recent. Soon it will be vastly easier and safer to, for example, drive from Mexico City to Acapulco, perhaps the most important and frequently traveled highway in Mexico.

Railroads are another sensitive issue. Many of the Mexican people view foreign control as a bad thing, so agreements between many U.S. railroads and their Mexican counterparts to help rebuild Mexico's rail system are underway. The theory is that this important new market will also be important for U.S. carriers interested in serving Mexico's market.

The airlines have been privatized and are thriving. More business travelers can now come to Mexico more economically and efficiently. And these privatizations have made it more economical for tourists to visit Mexico. Since tourist dollars are Mexico's third most important source of foreign capital, this privatization was well timed and thought out.

Agriculture

The government is now out of the coffee business, and other companies are soon to follow. Even the constitutionally protected ejidos (control of small parcels of farm land by "the people") are undergoing privatization-style changes.

Overall, hundreds of state-run businesses are now being returned to private ownership. The income from these privatizations has been well used to keep the ball

rolling and has done much to improve Mexico's economy as a whole. To you, this all means that these
programs and others prove Mexico to be a businessperson's heaven. The government believes in business,
wants the business community to prosper, and is putting
the future of Mexico into the hands of private business.
Also, specific opportunities in each industry have arisen
as a result of these privatizations, as we discuss in the
next chapter.

INCENTIVES

Government incentives for doing business in Mexico are
especially intended to increase or expand (1) foreign
investment and trade, (2) industrial technology and productivity, (3) employment, (4) tourism, and (5) production to less developed areas. As an initial step in
fostering an economic climate in which these programs
can occur, Mexico has overhauled its tax structure. Op-
pressive tax rates have been modified to make production competitive and investment attractive. Lower taxes
bring a smile to any businessperson's face and are an
excellent lure to Mexican investment. This tax reform is
continuing with more favorable regulations each year. A
prime inducement to foreign investment undoubtedly
has been the maquiladora program, which allows foreign companies to establish assembly plants in Mexico.
These plants import parts from the United States, Japan,
and Europe duty free; the parts are then assembled into
finished products and exported to the country of origin.
Duty is paid only on the value added. This program has
provided jobs for hundreds of thousands of Mexico's

workers and is a tremendously cost-effective method of production. Ford, Samsonite, General Motors, AT&T, and others are among the approximately 1900 maquiladoras now in production.

Tourism is another stimulus for foreign investment. The relaxation of restrictions on foreign ownership of coastal property and businesses related to tourism (detailed in Chapter 4) has introduced new opportunities. Generally, if a tourist-related project such as a hotel or shopping center will be of a certain size, will provide permanent employment for Mexican citizens, and will be in an area identified for development, 100 percent foreign ownership will be allowed. Also, you may effectively own coastal land through an irrevocable trust agreement. These concepts are relatively new and creating excitement within the tourism industry. To decide which areas are best for development, do your research and watch the giant businesses. Grupo Sidek doubled the size of Puerto Vallarta and now are building a huge project 60 miles south of Cancun. Stay up-to-date on the real estate news and visit the different areas to decide what will be best for your company.

Export companies are also receiving special tax and other incentives. So much new foreign trade is coming into Mexico that exports must be increased to keep a workable balance of trade. The rules are quite detailed, but the basic concept is that the higher the percentage of Mexican goods exported, the larger the incentives. This program must work to achieve investment in Mexico and more exports, so the government has wholeheartedly supported it.

Many other areas receive consideration to promote investment, including publishing, certain types of construction, and land deals for industrial parks. As price controls ease, further incentives for investment will increase. Basically, Mexico wants foreign investment, which increases employment, exports, and technological development. If your business plan fosters any combination of these elements, you will have opportunities in the marketplace. Look into specific programs and incentives for your industry.

LABOR

During the past 10 years, Ford Motor Company has invested more than $2 billion in Mexico. At this writing, they are backing that investment with an additional $700 million. Because automobile companies are labor-intensive, they are choosing Mexico. Nissan, General Motors, Chrysler, Mercedes, Volkswagen and others are all expanding their facilities throughout Mexico because of the cost of labor and the quality this labor turns out. The days of near-slave labor in Mexico are gone, replaced by an interesting system that, while favoring the worker in many respects, provides business overall with a stable and cost-effective labor force.

Mexico's Labor Ministry oversees the Federal Labor Law. Because of the rapidly increasing population, the country has a large, young, and eager labor pool under the ministry's jurisdiction. This sector of the government also oversees unions and their activities. Unions are the rule in most businesses of 20 or more employees. Unions are particularly strong in industrial sectors as well as in restaurants, the entertainment industry, and the media.

Once understood, the rules for Mexican workers are

relatively clear, in contrast to the ambiguities and excessive paperwork in the United States. As a result, unions and employers operate within certain fixed rules, and strikes are uncommon. For the entire package of regulations, contact the Mexican Labor Ministry, your local consulate, or your attorney, accountant, or consultant.

The minimum wage in Mexico is low, varying by region and type of worker. However, the employer must consider other required or customary benefits in the total cost of an employee. The low end of the scale at this writing is under $2 "fully loaded" per hour for the border maquiladora worker. The higher end is maybe $6 fully loaded per hour for established Mexico City workers. The employer must consider all the benefits that increase the base pay up to 100 percent, but as you can see, even when the benefits are available, labor is extremely economical in Mexico in comparison with that in the United States.

Consider the following as you prepare your business plan: mandatory profit sharing (the employee may inspect tax returns), medical and pension payments (similar to our social security), paid vacations, and a great deal of severance pay. Each business is now required to have training programs, to be reviewed by the Labor Ministry. Add a 5 percent payout to a national fund for employee housing and you have the basic package.

Except for some occasionally messy termination issues, Mexico's labor laws provide workers with a fair deal. Because employers and prospective investors can calculate labor costs with some certainty, business plans can be more precise. Strikes rarely occur, and workers stick to their contracts.

The bottom line is that Mexico can provide a huge

untapped labor pool that is readily trainable and cost-effective. The cost of living is lower, so labor costs are less. This resource will keep production cost-effective and allow Mexico to compete in the world market. This terrific labor situation is also a window of opportunity. Labor rates and availability are particularly good because past economic disasters left a huge percentage of Mexicans unemployed (and/or underemployed). As the economy continues to strengthen, more and more workers will have jobs, and the wages required to maintain a good work force will increase. Factor into your 10-year plan a significant cost-of-labor increase. Also factor in, however, that these workers are setting new world quality records for many manufacturers. Mercedes is expanding, and Nissan is even making cars in Mexico for reexport to Japan. Available and affordable labor is one more reason for you to consider Mexico.

ECONOMIC STABILITY

Mexico's miracles are all well and good, but will this new Mecca for business last? Can we count on Mexico's economy for the long run? Yes. Changes since the latter part of the 1980s have been no short-term fix; they have been broad and sweeping reforms, instituted in accordance with the goal of ever-increasing long-term economic stability.

Inflation has always been a problem for emerging economies. In 1988, Mexico declared it public enemy number one. Price and wage controls were instituted, and all fiscal decisions were made with a close eye on their inflationary effects. As a result, inflation in Mexico is now well under control. Long-term confidence in the continuance of this trend is evident in the emerging areas of real estate finance, financing of business equipment, and other financial tools that were previously unavailable under out-of-control inflation.

Diversification of industry and economy is another must for long-term stability. Mexico's fortunes and economy previously were tied to the roller coaster of international oil prices. Everything depended on oil revenues, and government policy was total reliance on this source of money, but no longer. Mexico learned its lesson in the 1980s. Diversification of Mexican business is proceeding rapidly. Privatization of state industry was a start. The government is spending millions to promote tourism, and its maquiladora program is bringing in foreign capital in amounts second only to oil. Incentives are in place for industry to move to open areas, and a new tax structure promotes economic diversification. Federal, state, and city planners are looking for new and different industries so that even local economies will not be dependent on any single source of money and jobs. Constant attention to diversification programs makes the long-term outlook for Mexico's economy an even safer bet.

What about employment? An economy cannot last long when there are no jobs for the people. Unemployment is still at an unreasonably high level in Mexico, but the rate is dropping fast. The maquiladora programs provide 500,000 jobs, and that number is rising. Terrific incentives, including tax and tariff breaks, are available for foreign investors who make permanent investments in Mexico that will provide jobs for Mexicans. Steadily decreasing unemployment is a sign of a growing and increasingly healthy economy.

Concentration of wealth is another issue. Until recently, Mexico's wealth was concentrated in only 5 percent of the population. As Mexico's economy continues to improve, the new middle class has the desire and resources to buy. As a direct result of the improving economy, now more than 50 percent of the people have the wherewithal to purchase discretionary consumer goods. More improvement in the economy will mean an even larger class of consumers. Widespread buying power is just another factor affecting economic stability.

Mass privatization programs have forced bloated and inefficient formerly state-run industries to become lean and competitive. Several sectors of Mexico's economy that have recently been privatized are critical to long-term economic stability. Communications, transportation, and financial institutions are now all in a competitive environment where management is responsible to shareholders to be profitable and competitive. Each of these privatized industries (and others) are making massive capital investments to rebuild industry infrastructure. Private industry is doing their part for economic stability.

More important to a nation's long-term stability are its people and its environment. Mexico's leaders have made commitments and are initiating programs to bring education within the reach of all citizens. On the environmental front, Mexico is taking bold steps to clean up its environment and planning for the future. So, yes, you can anticipate continuing economic stability. U.S. companies that have studied all these factors are showing their faith by investing billions of dollars in Mexico. Sam's Wholesale Clubs, General Motors, Blockbuster Video, Hewlett-Packard, Mercedes, and Canadian companies are representative of the hundreds of businesses within each

industry showing their faith in Mexico. With each commitment, Mexico's economy grows even stronger, with
more companies going for the long term, more jobs for the
Mexicans, and more foreign dollars to help with the balance of payments. The trend is toward a globally strong
Mexico; the momentum is unstoppable.

4

Business in Mexico: An Overview

We looked at Mexico's economy and culture; now it is time to study specific industries. This chapter is an overview of the important sectors of Mexican business: banking, tourism, communications, retailing, manufacturing, oil, and the stock market. Whatever your company's interests, it would be wise to consider the present status and future of all areas of Mexico's business world. Nothing happens in a void, so whatever your interests, they will be affected in some manner by most of what we discuss here.

Airlines

Nowhere are the winds of change and opportunity more active than in Mexico's skies. Mexicana is looking to expand to Latin American routes. Aeromexico is newly lean and competitive. Our U.S. carriers are less restricted under Mexico's new spirit of openness. Efficient transportation and a healthy airline industry are prerequisites for sustaining Mexico's rapid development.

Mexicana, Mexico's largest airline, was government owned but sold to private investors in 1989. Historically, Mexicana has been Mexico's premier airline, chosen by locals for its service and style. Mexicana's annual revenues are near the $1 billion mark, with 11,000 employees. The airline suffered some losses as a result of an ill-timed expansion into the United States when the U.S. economy was on a downturn, but the future looks bright. Mexicana's directors want to expand into the second hottest commercial airline market in the world: the newly booming Latin American routes. With proper long-term planning, significant financing, and a little luck, Mexicana will maintain its stature in the industry and grow throughout the 1990s.

Aeromexico, Mexicana's sole rival, went bankrupt in 1988. At that time their nickname was Aeromuerto—the airline of the poor and desolate—and rumors circulated that the pilots were government officials' children who liked airplanes. Like Mexico itself, Aeromexico is now a shining example of lean competitiveness, looking toward the year 2000. Trimming its staff from prebankruptcy highs, contracting with IBM for modernization of its reservation system, leasing rather than buying planes, and adding new planes each year have put Aeromexico on firm footing. Efficiency and service have radically improved passengers' image of Aeromexico. Rather than being considered a last-ditch alternative to Mexicana, Aeromexico is now the airline of choice for many of Mexico's travelers. Aeromexico is putting more emphasis on Mexico-Europe routes. Also, the airline is expanding its cargo and charter business (Aeromexico owns Mextur and Mexpress). With annual revenues slightly less than Mexicana's $1 billion, it is anticipated that Aeromexico will fund its Latin American and other expansion by entering the U.S. stock market very soon.

Mexico's burgeoning air transport needs have not gone unnoticed by U.S. carriers. The southern skies are looking ever more inviting as the U.S. airline industry "consolidates." The Mexican government's easing of restrictions is expected to continue as U.S. airlines test the waters. Long-range planners are considering Mexico not only as a lucrative new market but as a springboard to Latin America. Expect significant commitments from U.S. airlines in Mexico for the remainder of the 1990s.

Mexico's balancing act continues to work, with private enterprise taking the lead. For Mexico to sustain its impressive growth, effective, efficient air transport is as necessary as communications and roads. Aeromexico, Mexicana, some regionals, and now U.S. carriers are profiting and will continue to do so from this opportunity.

BANKING

Perhaps the most exciting (surely the most watched) changes in Mexico's business sector have been in banking. (Banking is incredibly interesting when the scope of changes to the industry is staggering.) First we discuss where the industry was before this transformation. Then we explain the privatization and consider what the new owners have in mind. Next we consider where the U.S. and Canadian banks fit into this new world and what the restrictions and opportunities are. Finally, we reach some conclusions about the future of banking in Mexico and consider the issue of competition.

In September 1982, President Lopez Portillo nationalized Mexico's banks. He won accolades from the country's left by denouncing bankers but weakened the economy and lost the confidence of business. Despite controls, during the 1980s the banks were often victims of fraud and mismanagement. They were frequently treated almost as the private accounts of certain industries. Mexican banks had little to fall back on, and no multibillion-dollar bailout program (as in the United States) was on the horizon.

The first step toward normalcy was President De La Madrid's returning of 34 percent of the bank stock to private hands. This action set the stage for what happened next. We know that Mexico needed a great deal of capital to get its economy back on the road to recovery. The oil industry was constitutionally protected, so Mexico could not sell off that asset. Mexico's leaders looked to the banks.

Mexico had (and has) 18 banks, each with 50 to 760 branches. All have been privatized. The largest, Banamex brought a sale price of $3.2 billion, and the next largest, Bancomer, raised $2.54 billion. Other banks, including Banca Serfin, Multibanco Comermex, and Banca Promex, also sold for hefty sums. Analysts anticipated total sales in the $6 billion range, but investors saw even more value. Ultimately, more than $10 billion have gone to the government from the privatization of Mexico's 18 banks, with sales prices averaging more than three times book value, ratios unheard of in our country.

Who is buying, and why are they paying so much? The two questions are quite related. Consortiums led by financial service companies are the main buyers. Acciones Y Valores was the leader in the Banamex sale; it is a major player in the stock brokerage business. Another brokerage, Probursa, paid the price for Multibanco Mercantil, and other financial service firms were the leaders of the other groups. (The big brokerage houses hold some 50 percent of Mexico's capital.)

Such interest from financial service companies is obvious: they know that the days of the superbank financial groups are coming. The United States has strict restrictions that permit banks to offer only a limited range of financial services, mostly pretty traditional banking. Mexico has no such restrictions. The government is even supporting the banks' entry into a wide variety of profitable businesses. The goal is for these super companies to compete worldwide and bring money and recognition to Mexico. The superbanks' vision is that they will offer banking, insurance, stockbrokering, factoring, foreign exchange, leasing, bonded warehousing, commercial banking, bonding, mutual funds, and much more. Thus the buying interest by the big brokerage houses.

What about competition? There is none. Although the United States and Canada have no restrictions on branch banking by Mexican banks, Mexico has severe restrictions on foreign banks that want to do business in Mexico. First, foreign banks cannot set up branches in Mexico, that is, no retail banking. More than 150 foreign banks have offices in Mexico, but only one, Citibank, which was "grandfathered in," has retail banking privileges. Second, foreign banks cannot own more than 5 percent of the voting shares of a Mexican bank, with total foreign investment limited to 30 percent.

As you can imagine, U.S. and Canadian banks are howling. The strong Mexican banks are buying up U.S.

and Canadian banks to set themselves up for future competition. Our banks are demanding reciprocity. Because Mexico does not really need the goodwill of U.S. banks and they want to protect their own, they are basically ignoring these demands.

The likely resolution to this conflict will be some sort of phase-in period for U.S. companies wishing to conduct retail banking in Mexico. Whatever the time period, U.S. banks will say it is too short since the superbanks are gaining strength by the moment. Mexican banks will want a longer period while they gear up for global competition without the nuisance of scrambling U.S. bankers.

The Mexican government is giving local banks a pretty free reign competitively but staying vigilant to prevent a recurrence of past problems. Individual ownership in Mexican banks will be limited to 5 percent without government approval and 10 percent with such approval. Institutional investors may own up to 15 percent of a bank's stock, but this limitation does not apply to financial holding companies. No more than 20 percent of a bank's loan portfolio may be to one borrower. Furthermore, under the new rules, banks cannot lend to employees, stockholders, directors, or their families. Also, no loans can be made to companies where bank directors hold equity.

Another item to know about in the banking field is Mexico's FONAPRE (Fund for Preventive Assistance), created in 1984 and also called the Banking Fund for Savings Protection. Headed by the Finance Secretariat, it is similar in some ways to our FDIC. At its option (unlike the FDIC) it may protect checking accounts, savings accounts, and other traditional deposits; it may not cover trusts, funds, and the like. The fund is maintained by a charge of 3 pesos for every 1000 pesos protected. At this time it is in healthy shape and is most conservative in its dealings with banks. Strict stock-collateralized transactions are their requirements for aid.

What does the future hold for Mexico's banking industry? U.S. companies will be permitted to engage in branch banking but will have to raise their capital locally. Prior to this new competition, Mexican banks will invest heavily in computer technology to make themselves as competitive as possible. Mexican banks will continue to get more than just a foothold in U.S. industry. They will continue to buy border banks to profit from the maquiladora industry, regain flight capital, and get local Hispanic deposits. The multiservice superbanks will soon come into their own and flourish along with Mexico's economy.

COMMUNICATIONS

Historically, Mexico was one of the very first countries to have a functioning phone system. Until the 1970s, ITT and its Swedish counterpart had the telephone concession. When the government began running Telefonos de Mexico (Telmex), things went downhill.

Lack of capital for infrastructure improvement during the protectionist years, coupled with the 1985 earthquake, left Mexico's communications system a shambles. A three-year wait for new phone service was not unusual, hampering both business and government. Telmex provides 5 lines for every 100 people, compared with 50 lines per 100 people in the United States. Mexico is the 13th largest economy in the world and yet ranks a tragic 83rd in phone lines per capita.

Recognizing that massive capital and technology injections would be required to provide a functioning communications system for Mexico, the government privatized Telmex in 1991. In the largest such privatization in the history of the world, a group led by Southwestern Bell and France Telecom has taken on the job. Everyone is watching, with no less than Mexico's development as a modern country at stake.

The new management's goal is to vastly improve service by a $2.5 billion annual infrastructure improvement program. The government is supporting these programs with tax concessions and rate increases. Even the formerly militant unions, with their 4.4 percent ownership of Telmex at stake, are pressing for the modernization of Mexico's communications. Telmex is now the fastest-growing communication company in the world.

The U.S. communications giant AT&T is also working on its own and with Telmex to improve transmissions between the two countries. Mexico is the second most frequently called country from the United States. Anticipating ever-increasing call and data traffic, AT&T has installed five cross-border fiber optic cables. Each cable can handle nearly 40,000 simultaneous calls, so these cables should be more than adequate well into the next century. On the receiving end, AT&T has also won some lucrative new contracts in building Mexico's new communications infrastructure. The U.S. company's share of a fiber optic network will connect 54 Mexican cities.

Confidence in the new Telmex is strong, as its stock more than doubled in price over 1991 and is still quite solid. At the present rate, Mexico's phone system should well exceed world averages by 1995. For those who do not want to wait, there are pricey alternatives. Telmex itself offers a fiber optic network and microwave system able to handle computer data. On a smaller basis, U.S. companies are setting up satellite links with Mexican satellites to transmit data to the home office. UPS and Mariott are among the first companies to take advantage of this service. In deciding which might be best, businesses balance the presently very expensive and unreliable phone service against the significant initial capital outlay for satellite hardware.

Telmex recently made a pact with Mexico's federal attorney general in charge of consumer complaints to respond to phone customers complaints within 72 hours. This is already a long way from past days when 6-month phone repair service was not unusual (and you had to be at home at whatever moment they came or you went to the bottom of the list!).

As an aside, keep an eye on 1996–1997, when the government has the option of allowing competing long-distance carriers into the picture. Expect Mexico's Telmex to modernize at a tremendous rate after this initial start-up period. Strong management, a tremendous need, and government, union, and international support ensure Telmex' continued success.

RETAILING

Retailing in Mexico, consisting primarily of grocery and department stores, is undergoing significant changes. The average Mexican citizen's standard of living is going up and will rise at an ever-increasing rate throughout the remainder of the 1990s. Consumers are now able to afford in increasing amounts and variety products that they earlier had no money for and that were unavailable because of trade restrictions. The handful of major retailers are racing to modernize and take advantage of new access to foreign products.

The main retail department store and supermarket chains of Mexico are Cifra, Comercial Mexicana, Grupo Gigante, and Soriana. The largest company, Cifra, has annual sales in excess of $2 billion. Recent stock issues by these companies have been tremendously well received, indicating investor confidence in Mexico's continuing economic growth.

U.S. companies are showing great interest in all this activity. Woolworth's Mexican subsidiary recently repurchased the 51 percent interest in their company that they had sold to outside investors in 1981 when retailing was very weak in Mexico. Other U.S. firms are entering a bit more cautiously as they remember problems K-Mart encountered in the mid-1980s as they entered the Mexican market.

Price Club and Wal Mart's wholesale divisions share similar strategies. The companies are teaming up with the established majors, and in joint venture arrangements they are going after a new market in Mexico's retailing. Wal Mart has linked up with Cifra to open retail clubs, operating in much the same fashion as their U.S. operations. Price Club is following suit with Comercial Mexicana.

To fully appreciate the brilliance of this strategy, you need to know one interesting fact of Mexican business. The giants mentioned above account for only one-third of Mexico's retail sales. The remainder of this multibillion-dollar sector of Mexico's economy is conducted by street vendors, marketplace vendors, and mom and pop establishments. What Comercial Mexicana and Cifra and their experienced U.S. associates are banking on is that these smaller vendors will use the retail clubs as their source of merchandise. This system of clubs is more efficient for the major wholesalers and gives small operations more access to a wider variety of merchandise.

Cifra's 192 stores, Comercial's 155, and Gigante's 97 are all looking to modernization and expansion as ways to stay competitive with each other. Price scanners, satellite hookups for credit card approval, and new management techniques are taking Mexico's retail business to new levels in up and coming Mexico. Anticipate more very major U.S. retailers entering the Mexican market. Furthermore, there is significant new opportunity for small and large U.S. wholesalers to supply this retailing boom. Consumers with the means are fueling the fire, and they want the U.S. products that they have long been denied.

MAQUILADORAS

The maquiladora program is vital to Mexico because it brings in foreign capital and provides employment for 500,000 Mexican workers. For U.S. companies, it is an unequaled opportunity to increase profitability through reduced cost of labor and economies of scale.

The word "maquiladora" has its origins in the old Spanish term "maquila," which refers to a mill owner who mills grain for others. Thus, the maquiladoras perform contract work under the "twin plant" idea, which we discuss here.

Historically, the United States and Mexico began

collaborating on labor issues via the Bracero program of the 1940s. Under this plan, Mexican workers were admitted into the United States for agricultural work. This project faded out in 1964; in 1965, the Border Industrialization Program formed the roots of today's maquiladoras. The 1983 Presidential Order for the Development and Operation of the Maquiladora Industry Program established the rules by which the maquiladora ventures are operated today.

A maquiladora is a Mexican assembly facility, often near a major U.S. market. Since Mexico absolutely must have foreign capital from exports to balance a trade deficit and to aid in the revitalization of its economy, special customs treatment and favorable foreign investment rules have been instituted. Foreign companies are permitted to import manufacturing machinery, raw materials, and component parts duty free to produce products in Mexico. Manufacturing facilities are built; Mexican workers at the facilities assemble the parts into finished products for reexport to the country of origin. Upon products' sale or reexport, duty is paid only on a value-added basis; that is, duty is based on the value of the product assembled minus the value of imported parts used in the product.

The maquiladora industry is big and getting bigger. Some 2000 plants manufacture more than $12 billion worth of products annually, using more than $5 billion worth of equipment. Many analysts claim that production in Mexico under these arrangements may grow fourfold by the end of the 1990s. Japanese giants Casio, Hitachi, Pioneer, and Sony are increasing their international competitiveness by assembling in Mexico. The U.S. companies Zenith, Ford, Westinghouse, Xerox, Mattel, and AT&T are among some of the huge multi-

nationals using the program. Although the larger companies get all the press, thousands of small- to medium-sized
concerns are racing to Mexico to benefit from the maquiladora advantages.

There are several advantages to producing in Mexico as a maquiladora. First and foremost is a tremendous
savings on cost of labor. Mexico has a large and under-
utilized youthful labor pool. Most companies save at
least 50 percent on labor, sometimes significantly more.

Two other benefits to producing in Mexico are that
some companies are required to have a "presence" in
Mexico in order to sell there (the same regulation applies
in South America) and that you can use the maquiladora
facility as a springboard into the Latin American market.
This third advantage is terrific for many companies; U.S.
Xerox sends half its production back to the United States
and half to Brazil.

There are three ways to enter the maquiladora program. One way is to form a subsidiary company (100
percent ownership is permitted). The advantage of this
method is that you control all production from start to
finish. If you want to try Mexican production with not
so much of an up-front capital investment, a second way
is to consider a subcontracting arrangement with an existing maquiladora. All the regulations and benefits still
apply, but there is a middleman. The advantages are fast
start-up and an inexpensive way to get educated about
the program. The third method is sheltering, whereby
you contract for finished products from an existing maquiladora that handles all labor and raw materials. You
lose some control, but you have no exposure beyond what
you pay the shelter operator. Sheltering is quite a big
business itself and something to be considered.

Before jumping into maquiladora production, you

must consider many factors. Labor costs are terrific and quality is now world class, but there is more to ponder. Weigh the cost savings from labor against additional costs incurred by producing in Mexico. These additional costs will vary by product and location of the home company, but they generally fall into the legal, travel, communications, transportation, customs brokers fees, duties, insurance, ability to finance, and management categories. If the scales lean toward Mexico for your product, the maquiladora program may be just the thing.

Many labor-intensive products are excellent candidates for Mexican production, including electronics (commercial and consumer), medical supplies, wood products, furniture, textiles, auto parts, auto components, cars, boats, toys, sporting equipment, ceramics, and home furnishing accessories. Recent rulings have made maquiladora production even more attractive. Mexico's Department of Commerce and Industrial Development's (SECOFI) approval process has been streamlined regarding time frame, equipment requirements, employment opportunities, and production schedule filings. Another great new ruling permits 50 percent of production to be sold in Mexico (subject to government approval case by case). Local suppliers are standing in line to serve the maquiladora market. A 4 percent local content requirement and a waiver of value-added tax for local suppliers make trade between the production facilities and Mexico's raw material suppliers quite favorable. A final regulation permitting export to a third-party country with import exemptions remaining intact makes maquiladora production an excellent opportunity for many companies.

Although many maquiladoras are located along the border, some 25 percent now are located in the interior of Mexico. Honda has a Guadalajara plant, and

AT&T will be assembling answering machines in that same city.

On a political note, as the border blurs, two issues arise in maquila discussions. One is the effect on the U.S. economy of moving south and second is the safety of capital in Mexico. The effect of the maquiladora and other free trade programs on the U.S. economy is that some jobs will be lost as companies seek Mexico's inexpensive labor, but countless others will be created, with this vast new open market boosting the U.S. economy. Also consider that many of these jobs would be lost to Asia if not to Mexico, and with them employment at the manufacturers' U.S. source companies. The maquiladoras are a long-run employment help to a strong U.S. economy and job market.

Regarding the safety of capital, look at the maquiladoras' record. The programs have enjoyed a 20 percent per year revenue growth each year since 1985. Many, many companies have already recouped their original capital investment and seen their profit margins soar. We never advise our clients to have all their eggs in one basket, but we are certain that investment of part of your resources in a Mexican facility is quite warranted. By becoming more labor-efficient, U.S. companies can now compete on the world market with Asia and the new Europe.

AUTO INDUSTRY

Several forces are combining to make Mexico's auto (and truck) industry front-page news. First, inexpensive labor has drawn manufacturers from the United States, Japan,

Germany, and elsewhere. Second, as Mexico's economy improves, the standard of living and the spending power of its citizens also rise. The workers and the new middle class all want that badge of success: a new car. Finally, Mexico's autoworkers are turning out products of a quality unsurpassed anywhere in the world. All this makes Mexico's auto industry one of the most exciting anywhere.

Issues

The explosive growth of the auto industry in Mexico has had significant political and economic effect in the United States. The U.S. labor unions claim that by manufacturing in Mexico, the U.S. automakers are depriving U.S. workers of jobs. The manufacturers respond that (1) to be globally competitive, they must take advantage of Mexico's inexpensive labor; (2) the jobs would be lost anyway to producers in the Far East, so it is better to pay workers who will use their paychecks to buy American products; and (3) increased production in Mexico provides jobs in collateral U.S. industries, such as auto parts.

Players

The Big Three U.S. auto companies are well represented in Mexican manufacturing and distribution. Ford, Chrysler, and General Motors are all committed to the extent of billions of dollars. Nissan is Japan's big player, and others are enviously watching their success in quality and sales. Germany's Volkswagen has always been strong; their production is up. Mercedes is expanding beyond truck production into luxury cars for the Mexican and (soon) U.S. markets.

The Industry

Mexico's auto industry, from manufacturing to exporting to sales, is the very picture of robust good health. What started some years ago as just a part of Mexico's maquiladora program is now a very significant part of Mexico's economy. Less restriction on foreign investment, significant reductions on import requirements, and much more has spurred this industry. In 1988, less than 500,000 cars were produced in Mexico. The year 1991 saw a significant increase, with 1 million cars, and the upward trend is continuing. And exports are up commensurately: 150,000 units in 1988 compared with 500,000 in 1992 (wait until you read our following forecasts). Local sales in Mexico are strong and continuing to rise. Behind closed doors (so as not to awaken the U.S. unions), automaking executives are jumping for joy.

Production for both local consumption and the booming export market is being done in hundreds of facilities in Juarez, Hermosillo, Chihuahua, Monterrey, Ramos Arizpe, Gomez-Palacio, Aguascalientes, Toluca, Mexico City, Cuernavaca, and Puebla. Volkswagen is making Beetles, Jettas, and other cars; Nissan is churning out Sentras, Minivans, and more. Ford started with Escorts, Chrysler with Ramchargers, Spirits, and Shadows. General Motors is manufacturing for the small car market, with a Buick being its largest. Mercedes is trying something new, and all the companies are doing great.

Trucks are big sellers in the local market as the Mexican economy and infrastructure are being rebuilt.

Trade, construction, and road building are keeping the
truck manufacturers working overtime. Labor is inexpensive, young, and eager to learn. The 100,000 plus
Mexicans working in the auto industry are presently
making just $20 per day while consistently breaking
company records for quality. Parts suppliers in the United States are benefiting from their increased sales and
production. But they are under increasing pressure by
the automakers to actually manufacture in Mexico;
border snafus and long-distance transport are causing
the major suppliers to consider doing so.

Forecast

The majors presently are not investing a great deal in
robotics and other expensive capital equipment; they are
relying on the economical and high-quality work force.
As wages rise, as they must, look for increased capital
expenditures.

By the year 2000, the Big Three will be producing
some 3 million cars in Mexico each year, with annual
exports of more than 1 million vehicles. Local sales will
be up fourfold from their 1985 level, and Mexico will be
one of the premier auto manufacturing capitals of the
world. Most major parts suppliers will be manufacturing and distributing in Mexico. Toyota and Honda, regardless of import restrictions and content requirements,
will be unable to resist this "can't fail" market. Labor
issues will have to be addressed as workers' wages rise.
By 2000, Mexico's auto industry will be ahead of its competition worldwide, as will be the rest of Mexico's economy. Are we bullish on Mexico's auto industry? Yes, and
quite rightly so!

TOURISM

Mexico is a tremendous tourist destination. Its coastline, resorts, restaurants, culture, archaeological sites, and variety offer something for everyone. For tourists, the country is accessible and convenient, with excellent transportation throughout. It has a strong tourism industry that projections indicate is still in its infancy. Huge projects, some guided and aided by the government, are making tourism and related activities a terrific opportunity for the 1990s.

Travelers from the United States make up 85 percent of the international travel to Mexico. Of the approximately 15 million U.S. visitors to Mexico each year, 90 percent are tourists. These visitors are the third largest source of foreign currency in Mexico as they spend some $6 billion annually. The government strongly supports the industry, not only because of this inflow of dollars but because of the thousands of jobs that are created and the investment in Mexico's tourist areas that is promoted.

Recent changes in investment regulations have eliminated many former obstacles to foreign investment. Now 100 percent foreign ownership of hotels and restaurants is permitted. And U.S. companies can participate on an equity basis with Mexican firms providing air and sea transport. Perhaps best of all, foreign ownership of coastal property is now possible through the use of automatically renewable 30-year trusts.

Private Development

More foreign visitors and more Mexicans able to vacation have created a demand for larger and more modern

vacation destinations. The government strongly supports private construction in the tourism industry, so
private companies, both Mexican and foreign, are going after their share of this almost unlimited development business.

Locally, Grupo Sidek, long one of Mexico's premier steel manufacturers, now has over two-thirds of its
assets in tourist-related projects and investments. When
the steel business slumped in the 1980s, the company
began shifting its energies and assets into the tourism
area, developing everything from hotels and condominiums to marinas. Sidek completed their Marina
Vallarta project in record time (doubling the size of
Puerto Vallarta) and is now hoping to duplicate their
tremendous success at Playa Del Carmen, south of Cancun. Innovators in the field, Sidek provides financing
for buyers in their condominium projects (an approach
until recently unheard of in Mexico) and then turns
over the debt as mortgage-backed securities. The low
record of default assures that they will be able to do this
again.

For the U.S. company wishing to get involved in
the development of tourist areas in Mexico, all this
means is that under new ownership rules you can develop land just as Grupo Sidek has done. But use care
in selecting your location because there are as many land
swindles in Mexico as there are in the United States.
Look carefully; for example, some areas of Baja, California, are effectively without a source of fresh water.
Once you have secured a location, your potential for
private development is almost unlimited. The insiders
are doing it, and as financing becomes more and more
of a reality for buyers, you can do it too.

Government Development

The National Foundation of Tourism (FONATUR) supports the government's policy of investment in tourism. Working with the Secretary of Tourism, FONATUR seeks private investors for certain designated projects and offers incentives for investment in those projects. FONATUR administers 19 tourist areas called megaprojects. These areas include Puerto Cancun, Punta Bono, Punta Ixtapa, Punta Nopolo in Baja, California, and the Bahias de Huatulco in Oaxaca. As Acapulco grew from a beach town to an international tourist attraction, so too will these developments continue to grow. Cancun has already surpassed Acapulco as Mexico's number one tourist destination. With FONATUR's promotion and continued foreign investment, the rate of growth promises to be phenomenal. For example, beautiful Bahias de Huatulco projects some 27,000 hotel rooms by the year 2020. No wonder hoteliers and developers are rushing to gain prime positions.

Recognizing collateral needs of these megaprojects, FONATUR is offering special incentives for investment in tourist-related areas. Marinas, golf courses, malls, services, parking lots, convention centers, dredging, and the like are all eligible for some significant incentives. FONATUR wants investors to do well and to promote a climate of major opportunity.

The financial incentives for investment are quite complicated and vary project by project, so check with an expert as to what is available in your particular area of interest. Possible incentives include inexpensive long-term loans, tax moratoriums or reductions, special labor exemptions, guarantees, and complicated but profitable debt for equity swaps.

Stop and think. Do you want to build yet another

hotel in Long Beach or Miami? Doesn't Mexico's wide open tourist industry make much more sense? Why fight with local regulations in the United States for one little space among thousands? Mexico is welcoming investors, builders, hoteliers, whatever. Learn about the tourism, construction, and development opportunities and where you might fit in.

OIL

Significant profit opportunities are developing in Mexico's oil industry. Historically, foreign investment in petrochemicals has been a constitutionally protected and emotionally charged issue. Still a political hot potato, the oil trade has been a significant source of revenue for Mexico's cash-poor economy. The now cash-stripped Pemex (Petroleos Mexicanos) is ill-equipped for the coming years and desperately needs a massive infusion of capital. Demand is now growing, and thus opportunity knocks.

Mexico is sitting on 50 billion barrels of known oil reserves. In the 1930s, U.S. and British petrochemical companies were doing the exploring and production. They grew fat and powerful. But the Mexican workers hated the slave-driving gringos, so in 1938 the people's president Cardenas told the 18 foreign oil companies that their assets were expropriated because of their arrogance and mistreatment of Mexican workers. Pemex evolved as the state-owned oil monopoly. As the working class cheered the action, Mexico's economy slumped and nearly failed, saved only by the advent of World War II. Even today there is a widespread feeling of nationalism regarding possible foreign investment in oil. Most of the Mexican people do not want foreigners involved, despite the industry's thirst for capital and the peoples' demand for gasoline. Politicians are trying to balance these issues, save the economy, and keep the populace satisfied.

On the surface, things seem OK for the time being. Mexico exported more than 7 billion barrels of oil last year, up 25 percent from the year before. Natural gas is being gathered rather than flared. Engineering is improving because of the recent elimination of the seniority system that put incompetents in high positions and held back true talent. In deregulation moves, the 70 strategic petrochemicals that were restricted to the government were reduced to 20. Pemex's oil exports bring in 30 percent of the hard currency coming into Mexico, and domestic demand is up yearly. So what can be wrong?

Since 1980, all of Pemex's revenues have gone directly into the country's treasury. Less than 25 percent is actually spent on the company's operations. Little cash is available for research, development, exploration, product improvement, and repairs. New capital expenditures have fallen 75 percent since 1980, and production has plummeted. The 1982 production of 3 million barrels per day dropped by 1990 to less than 2.5. Pemex' own estimates put output at 1.5 million per day by the year 2000 without additional capital investment.

Further problems plague this country that has the eighth largest pool of proven resources in the world. Mismanagement and outright fraud worsened the situation in the 1980s and early 1990s. With no competition, the giant monopoly Pemex grew to elephantine proportions, with 170,000 employees compared to Arco's (the same-size producer) 27,000. Add the burden of Pemex' providing 30 percent of Mexico's budget, and it is obvious that this giant is in bad shape.

Domestic demand for Mexican oil has been rising 7 percent per year. At this rate, by 1997 no oil could be exported at current production levels (never mind that production is decreasing). The disastrous effect of no more foreign oil dollars is all too apparent. Mexico already imports 100,000 barrels of gasoline per day. Something must be done now.

The government is finally dealing with their awkward problem. More than half the population believes that Pemex is grossly inefficient and riddled with corruption; still, cries of "No foreigners owning Mexico's oil!" are the rule. The politicians are working out ways to accommodate everyone.

Since 1986, many petrochemicals have been "reclassified" as nonstrategic, making foreign investment accepted. On the finance side, the government is working on creative borrowing arrangements from the United States that "implicitly" pledge future production against their loans. Note also that they are implicitly pledging the very same assets against recent Pemex bond issues.

Mexico's number one asset is going to be the savior of the country rather than the downfall. Significant changes are in store. Pemex' monopoly presently includes 8 working refineries, 21 petrochemical complexes, and sole control over crude oil imports and exports as well as wholesale gasoline sales. Privatization is coming, but perhaps packaged so that the populace will approve. Pemex itself will be broken up into several different groups, each group joint-venturing (they are already doing this with Mexican groups in the guise of "service contracts") with different foreign companies for more efficient exploration, production, and distribution. Soon thereafter, some of these smaller units will be declared non-strategic, and foreign ownership will begin.

As a first step, Pemex is franchising its service stations. The stations are still Mexican-only owned, and they must buy from Pemex, but this will gradually change as U.S. companies are allowed into the retail gasoline business (probably as early as 1995). Many significant changes in Mexico's petroleum industry will occur in the near future. The U.S. companies that are up-to-date in this constantly changing area will find vast areas in which to participate. Middle East unrest has brought to the forefront the United States need for a more local and stable oil supply. It is only natural that free trade will include to some extent a partnership to meet our need for oil and Mexico's need for capital investment.

STOCK MARKET

Mexico's stock market, the Bolsa Mexicana de Valores, has provided profit and excitement for many during the past 10 years. Now open to foreign investment, it is surely an opportunity not to be missed. Here we look at what makes up the Bolsa, discuss the funds available to foreign investors, consider some companies, tell you about a new exchange that is coming soon, raise some cautions before you invest, and make some forecasts.

A country's stock market often reflects the country's general economic conditions and investor confidence. Investors are very confident of the long-term continuation of Mexico's economic turnaround. For three successive years the Bolsa has been the top performing market in the world and is considered the hottest exchange of all emerging countries. With the market up some 600 percent over the past three years, no wonder there is so much excitement.

Located in Mexico City, the Bolsa is owned and operated by 25 Mexican brokerages. With approximately $100 billion in capitalization, some 210 companies are presently listed on the Bolsa. In 1991 alone, companies sold more than $4 billion in equity and another $1 billion in debt securities. Daily trading of nearly 100 million shares makes this a very active market, so active that trading times were recently extended by one hour to accommodate all the action.

Recent restrictions on foreign investment in the Bolsa have been lifted, but U.S. brokerages still cannot be members of the exchange. All purchases must also go through a member broker, and U.S. companies and investors cannot directly own shares. Foreigners can own shares through a trust mechanism administered by NAFINSA (the government development bank). Foreigners can also participate in this market through New York Stock Exchange–listed Funds and ADRs (deposit receipts). At this writing you can invest in four funds that hold combinations of Mexican securities.

The Mexico Fund, established in 1981, is by far the oldest. With some 20 million shares outstanding and a market capitalization of nearly $600 million, this equity fund invests in Mexican blue chips. This is the most conservative fund, investing only in equity securities and never placing more than 5 percent of its assets in any one issue. The Mexico Fund is presently expanding its capital base with an upcoming $125 million offering. This is the fund to consider if you are looking for long-term equity appreciation; it has an excellent track record for picking winners.

Another NYSE-listed fund is the Emerging Mexico Fund (MEF), which began in 1990. Its stated objective is long-term capital appreciation, but it is somewhat more aggressive in its approach than the Mexico Fund. Of its capital, 65 percent is invested in equity securities, 15 to 20 percent is reserved for short-term trades, and 25 percent may be invested in unlisted Mexican securities (private placements, joint ventures, partnerships). With 5 million shares outstanding and a $114 million capitalization, this fund also has an excellent (but chronologically shorter) record.

The Mexico Equity and Income Fund was also born in 1990. In many ways it is similar to the Emerging Mexico Fund, but it also invests a portion of its portfolio in Mexican convertible debt (it can invest up to 50 percent).

The Latin American Investment Fund is generating much excitement, and other funds are just now being formed.

In addition to the four funds, there are additional ways for you to invest directly in a number of Mexican companies. ADRs and ADSs are also available on the NYSE and the AMEX. These deposit receipts are effectively direct ownership of Mexican companies, but voting control is kept in Mexican hands through the abovementioned trust mechanisms. There are many choices among the ADRs and ADSs. Televisa (a huge television network), Tamsa, Grupo Situr (tourism), Telmex (communications), Empresas (construction), Grupo Synkro (panty hose, tennis shoes, makeup, sunglasses), Interceramica (40 percent of Mexico's floor tile market), and Cemex and Tolmex (it takes a lot of cement to rebuild a country's roads, airports, and housing) are among your electives. There are also companies in retail, construction, food, paper, mining, and electrical equipment, with many more to follow. Decide for yourself what part of the economy you think will be the biggest growth area.

Something interesting on the stock front is a new exchange that is being planned. It will provide for smaller emerging companies, that is, $3 million to $30 million in sales, an access to capital. It will be similar to our NASDAQ and might provide some true excitement for the knowledgeable investor.

There is a downside to this exciting market. First, although Mexico's Comision Nacional de Valores (their version of the SEC) is watching, Bolsa stocks have substantially fewer disclosure requirements than we are accustomed to in the United States. You can lessen your risk by sticking to ADRs because they must meet strict SEC requirements to be listed on U.S. exchanges. Second, only a few matters must be listed in a company's annual reports, but the more substantial companies list investment plans, acquisitions, mergers, and future problems. Third, overall valuation is a question. When the Bolsa first started getting hot, tremendous values were available, that is, shares selling substantially below the asset values of the companies. Now that values have caught up, you need to realize that you are betting on the growth potential of a company (or equity appreciation of a combination of companies when investing in a fund). As our final caution: remember that the Bolsa is still in its infancy and that there are huge amounts of capital spread over a relatively few companies. If there were a significant "correction" (broker's term for unexplainable disaster), there might be no short-term demand for your shares. As the market matures and more companies and investors spread the risk, the Bolsa will continue to strengthen.

The smartest way to minimize your risk as changes occur quite rapidly in growing Mexico is to make sure you use a broker specializing in Mexican securities and ADRs. Any brokerage can accommodate your order, but only a relatively few specific brokers specialize in this area (see the Resource Guide). Note also that a good broker can point out new opportunities in addition to potential problems.

What does the future look like for the Bolsa? Mexico's macroeconomic policies of free trade flows, decreasing public sector borrowing requirements, and control of inflation make Mexican stocks look good for the long run. Temper your expectations with knowledge of infrastructure problems, energy bottlenecks, and some lower profits as a result of the elimination of monopoly positions of Mexican companies as competition is allowed into the country. In this increasingly competitive environment, Mexican companies will have to spend otherwise-profit dollars on quality, research, development, and management. Overall, the stock market looks great for the long term and potentially profitable in the short term if you are sharp. Use a good broker and invest in Mexico's future.

5

Getting Started: A Checklist

Here is the chapter you have been anxiously awaiting. We discuss *exactly* how to begin doing business with Mexico. First we look at your choices: importing, exporting, franchising. . . . Next we consider how you can find your own special niche in this vast new market. We include special sections on how to research your area of interest and setting up a network of alliances and contacts to ensure your success. We consider the best way to find professional help and how to handle communications in a foreign country.

Now you are ready to go to Mexico. You will gain lots of knowledge from this book and your research, but you have to know how to put your information to work. You will learn what to do and what not to do when you get to Mexico. We also include tips on negotiating, sourcing, transportation and some miscellaneous information that will enhance your profitability.

YOUR OPTIONS

A U.S. or Canadian company (or individual) can participate in the Mexican market in the following nine basic
ways. Each option is studied in depth elsewhere in the
book.

Exporting to Mexico

One option is to export products to Mexico. In this
multibillion-dollar area there are literally thousands of
opportunities. This area is so important that we devote
Chapter 8 to exporting.

Importing from Mexico

Another option is to import products from Mexico. Labor-intensive items and agricultural products are your best
bet. You will learn how to select products in Chapter 9.

Assembling in Mexico

Many U.S. companies are subcontracting out their assembly work to companies in Mexico that specialize in such
assembly. This is the concept of sheltering, which we discussed in Chapter 4 in the "maquiladoras" section.

Owning a Factory Manufacturing for Export

This is the maquiladora opportunity. Basically, a U.S.
company owns 100 percent of a manufacturing facility

in Mexico. Equipment and components are imported duty free to Mexico; the product is completed in Mexico and then exported under very favorable conditions. Some 500,000 Mexican workers are employed in about 2000 maquiladora facilities.

Owning a Mexican Factory Supplying Mexico and South America

In most industries, a Mexican factory can be 100 percent foreign owned. This is the next logical step from the maquiladoras. A U.S.-owned factory can produce (in theory, using superior U.S. technology) products for sale to the Mexican market. Having your own factory in Mexico can vastly reduce your costs of sale to the Mexican consumers. Transportation costs will be less, and you can use Mexico's large and economical labor pool. Furthermore, you will then be in a better position to service the newly opening South American markets.

Your Own Mexican Company

As a foreigner, you are not restricted to just owning 100 percent of a manufacturing company; you can own 100 percent of almost any company you wish, whether you buy an existing concern or begin your own. There are three benefits: (1) The courts will treat you as a local because your corporation will be considered a Mexican entity. (2) Your company can take advantage of treaties between Mexico and other countries in areas where the United States has no such agreements. (3) Because of your proximity to South America, you can use your Mexican company to venture into South America.

Many countries in Central and South America are watching the modernization of Mexico with great interest. Using Mexico's continued success as a model, several countries have begun their own switch from protectionism to a liberalized economy and open world trade. Others are still at the watch, wait, and see stage, but Latin American interest in free trade is undeniable, and several agreements are already in place. Here lies yet more opportunity for the astute U.S. businessperson.

Since you are already looking at Mexico as the next phase of your business, you are way ahead of your competition, but remember that when you have your own Mexican company, you are considered a local and thus can take advantage of trade agreements between Mexico and Central and South American countries.

Mexico already has some trading agreements in place, and others are in the works, but this is just the beginning. As we mentioned, Mexico is not just seeking investment and trade from the United States. As the 1990s progress, country after country will continue economic liberalization and enjoy the benefits of more open trading policies. Mexico, with its geographic proximity and huge consumer base, will likely be the candidate that each of these developing countries will court as a trading partner.

Partnership/Joint Venture

This is an incredibly popular area. Companies such as Price Club and Anchor have been tremendously successful as a result of finding the perfectly compatible partner. You want a partnership that will create something greater than the sum of the parts. In the following chapter we study examples of this venture and warn you about some of the pitfalls involved.

Licensing and Franchising

U.S. franchises are quite popular in Mexico (more details about this in Chapter 7). If you have a licensable or franchisable product or service, this could be the greatest market in the world. Big population centers need everything and want things, particularly those things American. What is more American than McDonald's? And now even Taco Bell is opening in Mexico.

Investing in Mexico

Companies and individuals both are making direct investments in Mexico. With just a few restrictions you can own land and even participate in the stock market. If you believe in Mexico's future and growth, this is an option you will not want to miss.

Employment in Mexico

There is a demand for certain types of workers in Mexico, primarily bilingual white collar workers. As Mexico's economy goes global, so also grows the demand for managers and executives with global talents. Our Resource Guide lists a number of excellent recruiting firms in Mexico.

Your Choice

As you can see, there are countless ways to approach opportunity in Mexico. From the options listed, you should be able to determine which method or combination will best suit your purposes. Remember, you are certainly not limited to any one; some of the larger U.S. companies are accomplishing their goals using four or five different approaches simultaneously.

FINDING YOUR NICHE

We have given you a broad picture of Mexico, the land of opportunity for this decade. The country is immense geographically, and the scope of business endeavors mind-boggling. Now we begin identifying the specifics that might be right for you and your situation, that niche for which you and your company are best suited. The first step is to determine which of the following four categories applies to your situation.

Company Type 1

Type 1 is a specialized business with a limited or specific range of activities. For example, this company might manufacture pipe fittings or lamps or be a small hotel chain. This type of company should decide:

1. Can we expand our market into Mexico?
2. Is our product or service appropriate for Mexico?

3. Can we improve our product or service by using what Mexico has to offer?

4. Would Mexico be geographically suited to our company or any part thereof?

5. Are there government incentives or restrictions for our type of activity?

6. Can we import materials or products from Mexico?

7. Might a maquiladora facility work for us?

Of course, not all these inquiries are appropriate for every type 1 company, but they should help you pinpoint some specific opportunities. And these and other probing questions will raise other important issues for consideration in deciding if Mexico is a logical addition to your business plan.

Company Type 2

Company type 2 is still somewhat specialized but handles a broader range of activities, such as General Motors. Among GM's functions are manufacturing parts, manufacturing engines and cars, establishing dealer networks, marketing, sales, leasing, service, importing, and exporting.

Additional issues that the type 2 company must consider include:

1. Should we have a Mexican company, or would some sort of subsidiary be more appropriate?

2. Which of our activities might be more profitable in Mexico?

3. What combination of imported/exported parts and materials would be the most efficient and profitable at a new location?

4. Are there additional local markets we have thus far overlooked?

5. Are there additional export opportunities that arise from opening a facility in Mexico?

These and all the type 1 questions apply to your review of what Mexico might offer you. Your opportunities increase as the range of activities expands. The additional opportunities will require more extensive studies, but the benefits can be tremendous.

Company Type 3

Type 3 is an organization that already has a wide range of interests, such as Pepsico, which is now Mexico's largest consumer products company, with more than $1 billion in annual sales and still growing. The company's products and services affect a wide area of industry and government. Such companies have an even broader range of possibilities:

1. Shall we acquire land for future development as warehousing and manufacturing needs arise?

2. Are there new products specifically targeting the needs of the Mexican consumer? (Pepsico is a casebook study in success at this.)

3. Can we acquire existing compatible companies?

4. Are there opportunities both in Mexico and worldwide for joint ventures with others in the industry?

5. How can we expand or improve distribution in the industry?

The type 3 company is in a position to take advantage of many large-scale opportunities in this land of low-cost labor and 100 million consumers. Also remember that all the inquiries for types 1 and 2 are also appropriate and necessary here.

Company Type 4

Type 4 is often the smallest company—or perhaps even an individual—but has the broadest range of options. The type 4 company is just looking for entirely new opportunities for trade or investment. All the previous questions apply, and a great deal of general research will provide many ideas.

If any of the four types of companies represents your situation, Mexico has much to offer. For each type there are different opportunities; all types have a chance to join one of the boom economies of the 1990s.

RESEARCH

A critical step in beginning your Mexican venture is research, your fact-finding groundwork before beginning fieldwork in Mexico. Thorough investigation now can save money later and guide you to even more opportunities.

Research on U.S. businesses is easy compared to inquiries into Mexican business. Almost everything about U.S. companies is extensively chronicled in public filings, trade articles, and textbooks. You are traveling on new ground by venturing into Mexico. New horizons creating such opportunities also make your research somewhat arduous.

You have two ways of researching a specific area of business in Mexico. First, you can pay someone to do it for you (we cover this method in the later section called "Professional Help"). Second, you can do it yourself. We suggest that you research via a combination of the two methods. Get some basics on your own and then retain a professional to fill in the picture. Armed with your basic knowledge, you will be better able to select a competent adviser, and you will know which questions you want answered.

Here we discuss sources of information for your inquiries. Equally important and useful are the people you meet during your research. A business librarian, Department of Commerce associate, or someone at your local International Trade Center can be a wealth of information if they take an interest in you and your project.

Let's begin at the most business-oriented of your local libraries. A major university business school is perfect, but any library can get you started. Newspapers, magazines, and trade journals with articles about Mexico contain the most up-to-date information. These articles are often cross-referenced by subject matter. Explore your topic and ask for help. Listen. We also have found the *Periodical Index* invaluable; some specialized publications you never dreamed of exist, some of which provide great leads for your project.

There are few books on the subject of doing business with Mexico, so your research will be limited to publications and different trade, business, and government agencies. We look first at periodicals and then at agencies and groups that can help you. Some publications, which we list and discuss here, are extremely valuable and important for you to know about. Others are in the Resource Guide. This list is *not* exhaustive.

El Financiero, Mexico Business News (International Edition in English)

This publication is a must if you are going to be doing business in Mexico on a continuing basis. It is also most helpful for your initial research. Its weekly international edition, printed in English, is similar in format to that of the *Wall Street Journal* or *Barrons*. It covers new rules and regulations, economic news, politics, stocks, trade, and much more. For general business news and insightful forecasts on various sectors of the Mexican economy, nothing compares to it. It is sometimes hard to find but well worth the effort.

Business Mexico

Business Mexico is the monthly magazine publication of the American Chamber of Commerce of Mexico. It publishes in-depth articles on U.S. companies doing business in Mexico as well as analyses of issues relating to United States/Mexico trade, business, and investment. This is a good way to keep an eye on the pulse of U.S.

business in Mexico. It is available at some newsstands or
by subscription.

Twin Plant News

If maquiladoras are your area of interest, this is your
publication. This monthly magazine covers specifically
all the news on the 2000 maquiladoras operating in Mexico. Who is doing what? What are the problems, solutions, and new opportunities? What about the environment, labor, new regulations, transportation, and taxes?
For those interested in manufacturing in Mexico, *Twin
Plant News* can be a goldmine. An important feature of
this publication is a listing of upcoming trade confer-
nces and industry shows and meetings.

Export Today

Here is a fine publication of general interest to the exporter. This monthly magazine does not cover just Mexico, but it has a great deal dealing specifically with that
subject. It is great for your research and keeping up-to-
date on exporting worldwide. Finance, economics, and
an excellent networking section make *Export Today* a
good value. The listing of upcoming trade shows and
international events of interest to the exporter is wonderful. *Export Today* is widely available at newsstands
or by subscription.

Business America

This U.S. government publication in magazine form is
published monthly and is often available at universities

in the Government Documents section (also available by subscription). It contains some interesting articles on international trade, but discount its predictions and forecasts a bit because it tends to promote whatever the U.S. government is supporting at the time. It does, however, list other valuable resources that you might not find elsewhere.

World Trade

World Trade is a monthly magazine that addresses many interesting issues companies face when going global. It features real-life stories and articles on companies that are doing well in international trade as well as quite a bit on Mexico and South America. Slightly off the beaten path, the magazine has carved out its own niche in international trade news, much as *Forbes* has in U.S. business. *World Trade* has amusing commentary, practical advice, case studies, and information often unavailable elsewhere. It is available at many newsstands.

Journal of Commerce and Commercial

This newspaper-style weekly is quite surprising. Primarily concerned with shipping, it is a wonderful resource for transportation-related issues. It often seems to also get you-heard-it-here-first news on nontransportation items. To save money on transportation, discover what is coming next, and keep up with the competition, this "only known by insiders" publication is great. Check the business libraries, or subscribe to it.

Forbes, Fortune,
The Economist, Business Week

All these magazines include articles on both Mexico's general business environment and specific companies and issues. Your research will not be complete without checking their offerings. The *Periodical Index* at the library will steer you to back issues relevant to your area of interest.

Newspapers

Depending on where you live, your newspaper may or may not consider business in Mexico an important issue. Consider the following because they have many articles on Mexican business: *Los Angeles Times, San Diego Union, San Antonio Times,* the Dallas and Houston papers, *Arizona Business Gazette, Los Angeles Business Journal, Crain's, San Diego Business Journal, San Antonio Business Journal, Dallas Business Journal, New York Times, Washington Post,* and others. In other words, consult the newspapers from areas whose local economies are significantly affected by business in Mexico.

Industry-Specific Publications

Every industry has its own particular publication, such as *Women's Wear Daily* for apparel, *Restaurant News, Travel Weekly, American Banker, Home Furnishings Weekly,* and *Automotive News.* Once again, the *Periodical Index* and your librarian can steer you to a publication in your area of inquiry. Various groups and organizations also put out a number of newsletters and one-time publications.

Public and Private Offices

Certain public and private offices exist to encourage just our type of activity. Here we look at a few of the most important; others are in our Resource Guide.

U.S. COMMERCE DEPARTMENT

These departments are funded by your tax dollars, so use them. Each state has at least one office, each office being divided into the many services that the Department of Commerce provides. Here is a terrific place to start once you are armed with some facts and figures from other research. The departments can vary in helpfulness, depending on what you are asking and to whom you speak. Ask lots of questions. A helpful Department of Commerce associate will know of many resources that you might not otherwise hear about. They also have some interesting newsletters free for the asking, for example, *Latin America/Caribbean Business Bulletin.*

AMERICAN CHAMBER OF COMMERCE IN MEXICO

With offices in each major population center in Mexico, this is a very valuable source of information. A private organization, supported by the dues their members pay (including many U.S. businesses in Mexico), the stated aim is to serve U.S. companies entering the Mexican market. Do not skip the American Chamber. Check out their publications; they will give you an idea of the tremendous scope of their knowledge.

YOUR STATE TRADE COMMISSION
OR EXPORTING OFFICE

Many states, in the interest of providing expanded markets for their citizen companies, have offices to provide information for businesses interested in international trade. Some states, like California, even have such offices in Mexico. Call your state capital and see what your state offers. If they offer nothing, call another state that is active in Mexican trade.

MISCELLANEOUS FEDERAL OFFICES

Besides the Department of Commerce, many federal offices are willing to help with your specific inquiry. Depending on your area of interest and the size of your company, the Department of Agriculture, the United States Small Business Administration, U.S. Customs, and many more offices are funded by your tax money, so get your money's worth. All these groups can tell you about different programs and offices, so just keep calling until you find what you want.

Other Resources

A number of sourcebooks for Mexican contacts are available. They are usually quite expensive, so choose wisely (a typical bank sourcebook listing all importers can cost $350 or more). Also, we have found that unless these sourcebooks are very current, they are of little help, so watch not only the dates of publication but the dates that the information was gathered—things are changing rapidly in Mexico.

The Mexican Consulate can be a tremendous source of advice, but do not waste this contact. It can be quite valuable for something specific. You may need this resource later on in your venture, so be tactful.

Finally, and quite important, there are professionals available to help with your research. The most useful are specialists in Mexican business rather than international trade in general. You will learn how to select these people in the "Professional Help" section, but for now remember that these experts have already formed their alliances and so can learn from one phone call what you have been unable to unearth in a month.

We hope you understand the importance of research. You are inquiring into opportunities in a different country and culture. This book will guide and steer you around some rough spots, but nothing can take the place of information gathering at the outset of your project. Later you will find that your time and money have been well spent.

ALLIANCES AND CONTACTS

You have done your research; you have narrowed your focus. Now it is time to get things done. There is an easy way and a hard way to function south of the border—we discuss both. You will learn how to establish your own associations and learn the rules of conduct you will be expected to follow.

To fully appreciate where we are going in this section, you should understand that Mexicans are almost genetically different from us in one respect. They have a networking gene that puts our concept of contacts to shame. We will explore this concept a bit, but remember that our point is that once you are plugged into the

Mexicans' network, your project becomes easy and fun, your success assured.

In the United States, the adage "It's not what you know but who you know" is often repeated. Practically speaking, the adage is relevant in business but certainly not pervasive in our commercial world. In contrast, Mexico's business and government operate almost exclusively on this slightly different rule: "What you know is important, but you will go much further because of who you know." All this is closely related to the "We only do business with friends" concept we discussed in Chapter 2. Beginning with this "Who you know" concept, let's look at the hard and easy ways of doing business in Mexico.

Level 1

At level 1 of the business world you do your research and fieldwork. You are honest and persistent, and your project is sensible—the Mexican government welcomes your investment and trade. Everyone is very polite, you enjoy the country's favorable economic climate, and the venture is profitable. Level 1 is good as far as it goes, but there is an easier way.

Level 2

Level 2, once you understand it, will expand your opportunities quickly and exponentially. This is the who you know level in a country that keeps its guard up until it is discovered "whom is known." This is the level at which you plug into your associates' huge network of acquaintances and get that key to the country, known in

Mexico as the personal referral. Most business relationships begin with trust and respect. And respect is built
over time as you prove yourself. The personal referral in
Mexico leapfrogs you to a position of respect. You have
the stamp of approval from an insider.

Personal referrals (entrance into the network) are
extended only after you have established your good character and credentials as a "fine person." This is the importance of alliances. After the initial phase, you will
find that almost every businessperson you deal with has
a mind-boggling network of acquaintances. Mexico is a
very social country; outsiders call it clubby, insiders
think of it as an extended family. As years go by,
hundreds of relationships are formed almost effortlessly;
people keep in touch regardless of time or distance. In
the United States, networking is pushy, but in Mexico it
is social, automatic, and part of friendship.

Once you establish yourself at level 2 of Mexican
business, doors will open for you. Often you will find
more doors that you did not even know existed opening
and welcoming you to success in this interesting world.
Everyone knows someone who can guide you the right
way. Petty jealousy is unknown in Mexico's business/
social world. Your friends' allies will go out of their way
to help you succeed and give you referrals without reservation. Your success is now of great personal importance
to them, your failure unthinkable at this level. The extent of this practice is almost incomprehensible until
you become involved, at which point it seems natural
and you wonder why the rest of the world is so un-
friendly.

With time you will establish your own alliances.
Consider retaining an expert at the outset to speed up the
process.

Rule 1

Now for the rules governing your newly established network. Follow them carefully because a breach of decorum can close doors forever! Rule 1 is pure etiquette. Do not abuse, overuse, or be pushy about a request for assistance or referral. Such a request is taken seriously and should not be made for a trivial matter. Furthermore, your own reputation is now on the line along with the integrity of your venture. Overuse of a friend's goodwill is also a business sin. The Mexicans are a giving people, but do not take advantage of them. Pushiness is also unacceptable in requesting referrals. If your ally is hesitant to pursue an inquiry, do not press the matter. There can be 1000 reasons for this hesitancy, any of which can cause embarrassment or loss of respect for you or your friend.

Rule 2

Rule 2 involves financial remuneration for these referrals. This is a very delicate matter at best; you must be very careful to avoid offense. Your friends truly wish for your venture to work well. They will assist to the degree they feel comfortable, with no expectation of financial benefit to themselves. Offer none at this point, but do the right thing later on. If their assistance proves invaluable and your business benefits tremendously, a fee or some other consideration should be given (not simply offered, as they would be obligated to refuse). Again, this is all very delicate, but follow your instincts and the right thing will become automatic. Once again, an expert can advise you about the right thing to do.

Business is stylish and fun in Mexico if you get into the rhythm. Alliances are a large part of the activity. Pettiness is not in the Mexican's vocabulary, and prosperity for all one's friends is a common goal. You will need contacts and alliances to succeed in Mexico to any great degree. A tremendous alliance can happen almost by accident, from something as simple as a personal referral from a friend at the consulate. Obviously networks operate at different levels and in different areas, but there is so much interchange that you will find it easy (once you are admitted and approved) to cross over into other networks with ease.

FIELDWORK

Now it is time to get down to business. You are going to visit Mexico. All the research you have done and the contacts you have made are useless unless you put your knowledge into action. And it is just impossible to do business with Mexico without going there.

Let's consider the cost. Telephone calls to Mexico often cost $20 to $40 each (you will learn in Chapter 10, "Business Etiquette," that pleasantries must be discussed before business, even at $2 per minute). For the price of a few phone calls you can fly to Mexico and begin your business in person. So shop for rates, buy your ticket a little in advance, and you will find your flight most economical.

There are considerations other than just cost. Mexicans pretty much do business only with friends. Well, unless you have the verbal charisma of Will Rogers, you cannot make friends on the phone. Also, the networking aspect of Mexican business is impossible without several (minimum) face-to-face meetings. Business in Mexico is very person-oriented, you want to give the businesspeople an opportunity to take your measure (and you can take theirs at the same time). Thus you must travel to Mexico to get started. Forget the beaches, shopping, fine dining, and culture—pack your bags, roll up your sleeves, and head south.

About one week before leaving, you should phone those people you want to meet. Do not make a firm appointment, but announce the length of your stay and make sure your contact will be in town then. Explain that you will call for an appointment when your schedule is finalized.

You now have arrived at a Mexican airport. Welcome to the Third World. Do not rent a car during this fieldwork stage; take a taxi (covered in the next section, "Negotiation"). A taxi is quite inexpensive and often available on a daily basis. Your driver sometimes turns out to be an interesting alliance. A loyal, clever, and industrious driver can be invaluable, but remember, the other kind of driver also exists.

Go to the hotel you carefully selected. Prices and quality vary widely, and a higher price does not necessarily indicate increased quality. Get the best rate by asking or calling ahead. Rates even within one hotel can vary quite a bit. The knowledgeable pay less. Also remember that the Corporate rate is not necessarily the lowest. Find out where the local businesspeople stay and you will be well served at a reasonable price. Do not tolerate the last-minute price fluctuations that, occasionally, an enterprising clerk might try. If the clerk does try, demand to see the manager, and the unscrupulous individual will suddenly see his mistake.

Now you're on site. An easy way to supplement your research at this point is to consult the local phone directory for who else offers services and products in your field of interest. Often you can find some smaller suppliers that do not have the resources to get their name out in the United States. A choice of more than one supplier can mean better prices, so a quick scan is well worth your while. And the more sources and services you investigate, the more knowledgeable you will be when it comes time to negotiate a contract.

Before making your first appointment, enjoy a bit of the local culture. Yes, this is a business necessity. We point out in Chapter 10 that the first questions you will be asked at every business meeting are "How long have you been here?" and "What have you done?" You will be considered a culturally unappreciative cretin if you have not yet visited a museum or other historical site.

Now, call two of the businesses you wish to consider. Set a morning and an afternoon appointment. Two or perhaps three appointments in one day is the maximum for two reasons: (1) meetings in Mexico tend to be longer than in the United States because of the obligatory social talk, and (2) you need extra time for scouting collateral opportunities.

At your meetings, follow the rules of business etiquette discussed in Chapter 10. At all times during your Mexican visit, question, listen, and look. Probing questions requiring in-depth answers will get you more information than those requiring a simple yes or no response. Listen to the answers, not only for the information offered but for what might be between the lines. For example, consider the response "Usually the customer pays the shipping." Understanding the word "usually" can save thousands of dollars over the course of a year.

Remember also to look around during your meeting. Your host will undoubtedly take you on a tour of his facility, and you should be most complimentary, no matter how humble the place is. Look around for affirmations or inconsistencies. For example, if the company promises to deliver 10,000 completed lamps to you in 30 days and there are four workers in cramped quarters doing the assembly, you will be glad you looked.

It goes without saying that during your meeting you are in a great position for making an alliance. If appropriate, you might ask if your host knows sources for the other products and/or services you seek. This is less than a personal referral, but new sources provide new opportunities. Of course, do not ask for other producers or suppliers of his particular service.

Do not expect to conclude your business at this meeting. Should you be in too much of a hurry, your counterpart might be concerned. Even if you are ready to buy, this is not the time. Also, if you are offering to sell him something, do not try to close the sale at this time for the same reason. The rule of thumb is: the earliest you will pursue a final contract will be by phone later in the week or at another meeting before returning to the United States. Often business is not concluded until many months later. This is particularly frustrating for a business trying to break into the market, but your patience will pay off in better prices and terms.

After your meeting and before the next one, look at the surroundings. Often many businesses in the same or associated fields are located near each other. Have your taxi driver take you around. Pay attention. We have found some of our best sources and customers in just this manner. Many phone books are out of date regarding fast-growing businesses, so you might miss new companies altogether. Time spent in apparently aimless wandering often will provide benefits you have not yet even considered.

Also remember that, at all times you are looking for the source, either the (1) actual producer of the product or service you require or (2) ultimate purchaser/user of the product or service you are offering; you do *not* want the middleman. In a nation of millions of middlemen, many of whom are related, this can be an extremely delicate affair. You might consider using a professional to act as your middleman to avoid embarrassment. Properly handled, you may save up to 50 percent on your cost or add 50 percent to your profit, but the slightest mistake at this stage can doom you to failure. As an example, imagine your first meeting. You want to find a source for boxes. Your host shows you through a small warehouse, where you notice that each box is labeled Produced by Boxcar. Obviously you need to know who Boxcar is before you can make a commitment, but you can hardly ask your host. Do not even be tempted to inquire because doing so might prove awkward. You can find out on your own. Things can go wrong, if say, Boxcar is owned by your host or his brother. By finding the factory itself, you will certainly lose respect, which is fatal at the negotiating stage. Look for the source but tread cautiously.

You can also drop in on the U.S. government and/ or state offices in the areas you visit in Mexico. These people are on site full time and often have leads for just your field. The state of California, for example, has an incredibly useful field office for you to visit.

As you can see, fieldwork enables you to meet face-to-face with people. You can analyze, make alliances, and establish respect. Also, over the phone it is difficult to see the physical capabilities of any operation, a critical piece of information for later decisions and negotiations. Happenstance is another benefit of fieldwork. Luck happens to the industriously busy. You will often stumble across a major new alliance, source, or opportunity. And fieldwork can be great fun as you discover new friends, new places, and that pulse-quickening thrill of a stable new source of profit and opportunity.

NEGOTIATION

You have completed your research, made some contacts, and are on site, ready to deal. Now is the time to open negotiations with a potential supplier, seller, provider of services, or new customer. Whatever the situation, you are prepared. You have already learned as much as possible about the industry, the business climate, your host's competitors, and the business with which you are now entering discussions. All this will pay off in real-dollar terms as you begin the most critical phase of your Mexican venture: negotiating. Negotiation is an art in today's business. Volumes have been written about it and courses taught; what follows are important threads that run throughout this art in Mexico.

Vocal Bartering

Before all else, remember to not confuse business negotiation with the type of vocal bartering that takes place between market vendors and luau-shirt–clad tourists. The latter type of bartering is simply a rite of tourism, practiced by visitors and tolerated and sometimes encouraged by street sellers. Loud and offensive conduct is unwelcome and most inappropriate in business negotiation. Do *not* lose all manners and evidence of good breeding the moment you cross a border.

Social Talk

Social talk always comes before business. Families and social concerns are what really matters, and you must acknowledge this concept. It is a fundamental precept of business in Mexico and should not be taken lightly. No matter what your time constraints, never forget this rule; you will be in a much better position speaking of your families for 15 minutes and returning later than skipping the formalities. Not only is social talk evidence of your good upbringing and values, it shows that you are not in a rush. The party in a hurry always loses in negotiations. Time your visits, appointments, and business to allow for this time of enjoyable conversation.

Check Your Concessions Before Offering Them

Entirely too many otherwise solid transactions and partnerships have failed at the inception because of this problem. When you are negotiating on home turf here in the United States, there are many concessions you can make, such as those involving transportation, packaging, advertising, promotions, add-ons, and trades. You must be careful in Mexico, which has significantly different sets of laws, regulations, and tariffs. Many of these are based on historical precedent rather than modern-day reason; that is, they make no sense whatsoever to a modern businessperson. Do not be unduly concerned about the rules in Mexico, but do be knowledgeable regarding your transaction. As you most likely know from the law of contracts, the slightest impossibility or illegality in a carefully negotiated agreement can void the entire transaction. Do your research and/or check with your professional advisers about laws affecting your area of interest.

Bring in a Professional

This is the one time during your setup for doing business in Mexico that you should hire an attorney, consultant, accountant, or some combination thereof because one simple clause won or lost in negotiations can cost many thousands or even millions of dollars over the life of your agreement. Clauses relating to changing laws, currency revaluations, schedules for increases or decreases in prices, availability of supplies or raw materials—all these can keep a wonderful agreement functioning during the most trying of times. The experts available have been doing this long enough so that they can anticipate problems that you, the newcomer, could not imagine. Bring in help, and do not be cheap; you will pay much more in the long run for a small economy now. This rule applies not only to the five-year multimillion-dollar contract but also to the small player negotiating for just a few container loads of merchandise.

Be Prepared to Walk Away

You are in Mexico, you have been looking forward to this for a long time, and everyone at the home office is counting on you. All these factors can make it hard to walk away from a negotiation, but you must overlook them. Certainly you should exit negotiations gracefully, but your mind-set must always be that if you cannot negotiate a profitable deal, it is time to leave. Any experienced businessperson can spot desperation, so do not reveal a weak side. These people are really quite sophisticated in the ways of business, so pay attention here. If you get boxed into a corner from which you cannot profitably extricate yourself, it is often better to leave and try another approach later than to risk offense or loss of respect by your inflexibility.

Silence

Good use of silence is an excellent negotiating tool anywhere, but in the subtleties of Mexican business it can be priceless. Used in your favor, it can bring unasked-for concessions; if you are unprepared, it can be used against you with devastating results. Basically, never rush to talk. Silence never killed anyone, and those who rush to fill it are often giving away the store. For example, your host says "We can probably give them to you for $4 per unit." This is a terrific price because you were expecting to pay $8 or even $10. Your instinct is to say "done" before they can change their minds. Your best play, however, is to simply sit there for a minute saying nothing (this minute can seem like a year). Very often your host will interpret this silence to mean that you are expecting additional things to be offered. Eager to please and uncomfortable with the silence, he, like many in a similar situation, will jump in and say "Of course that includes shipping to your California warehouse" or "Maybe we can do $3.75 if you commit to a sufficient quantity." The real experts at negotiating use this technique as a powerful weapon, so be ready for it and use it in your favor. Especially in a bicultural situation, silence will be interpreted (often wrongly) as inattention or disinterest. Do not make that mistake; do not be scared of a little quiet.

Never Put All Your Cards on the Table

Particularly in Mexico, this rule is true. The Mexicans' interesting sense of time enables them to never be in a rush to reach an agreement. It is probably unthinkable to them that any agreement of substance can be reached in a short time. The "I'll make my best offer first and they can take it or leave it" technique works even worse in Mexico than in the United States. Leave the table with at least one card left to play. On many, if not most, occasions where we have been involved in negotiations for our U.S. clients, the phone rings back at the hotel with a "We've thought it over and we're ready to grant your request if you can make just some small concession." We always save some grand-sounding but not necessarily substantive ace to offer them at this point. Face is saved all around, and there is another profitable transaction for our client.

Do Not Burn Bridges

In Mexico, it is of the utmost importance that you not burn bridges. This is a good rule everywhere, but critical in Mexico. As you know from the earlier discussion of alliances, Mexican business and government comprise a tightly knit community where everyone is in some way connected to everyone else. You may assume that the fellow you offend during negotiations will turn up elsewhere in a position to make you humble; it never fails. So no matter how outrageous the demands, exit gracefully and with your bridges intact.

Keep Negotiations Impersonal

Closely related to the concept of not burning bridges is the rule of keeping yourself (as an individual) removed from the negotiations. Whenever possible, refer to your associates. Consider the following illustration: "You're absolutely right and I can see your logic, but I'm afraid my associates might misunderstand your reasoning. Perhaps if we could offer them some token price concession they would understand your good intentions." By avoiding personal disputes in possibly irreconcilable areas, you leave open the option of retreat without loss of respect. This rule of negotiation applies equally whether you are on the buy or sell side of the transaction. This strategy is true everywhere but excellent in Mexico, where respect means more than money.

Do Not Gouge

In the win-win negotiating philosophy, both sides come out ahead. Because of Mexico's past economic problems, you might find yourself in an unduly advantageous bargaining position. If so, you will earn respect and long-term goodwill by striking a favorable but *fair* trade. In a country where goodwill is measured in generations, this is a terrific plan. If you take undue advantage of a person or company, resentment will build throughout the relationship and quality will suffer. Be fair, earn respect, and gain greater long-term rewards. Mexico's economy is improving at such a rate that you may find yourself the one in the weaker position later, so you will be glad you have the reputation for fairness.

PROFESSIONAL HELP

Here is some great news that should make you feel quite secure in beginning a new venture south of the border: Whatever your area of interest, professionals are available to help you. For business advice, general or specialized, there are consultants in every field. Legal information is available through a number of competent U.S. or Mexican firms. If your questions pertain to tax, audit requirements, financial compliance, whatever, use a qualified accounting firm. Professional help is the correct route to follow. Avoid problems later and seize opportunities now. Business requires economy of both money and time: find those professionals who can save you both.

One short warning here. Mexico's economy and opportunities are growing at so frantic a pace that there are many self-proclaimed experts popping up in all the fields. The experts want their little piece of the action. You should not have to pay for their education, nor should you rely on the advice of the inexperienced. In selecting your professional, work through a personal referral, or at least ask many questions regarding specific experience. On the other hand, if you are fortunate enough to work with the correct professional for your field, you can avoid many problems and find opportunities that perhaps you would not have found otherwise.

Attorneys

A number of legal issues must be considered when you begin doing business in Mexico. Do you want to form a Mexican company? What are the permit requirements? What are the labor rules? What are the regulations for a joint venture? These and many other legal issues are the province of an attorney experienced in Mexican laws.

Should you hire a Mexican attorney, or one in the United States? In any event, you will need an attorney licensed to practice in Mexico. Finding one is easier than you think. Some U.S. firms have opened offices in Mexico, to better serve their U.S. clients. While their attorneys are not licensed to practice in Mexico, they associate local lawyers on a case-by-case basis. Your alternative is just as attractive. If you know others involved in the Mexico trade, ask for a referral to an attorney in Mexico, or your consultant can find the appropriate legal adviser for your business.

One thing to watch out for. Many attorneys in the United States hold themselves out as experts in international law. When you hear these words, be cautious. What you will require is an attorney specifically knowledgeable about trade with and investment in Mexico.

As you do your research, you will find articles written by attorneys or specific lawyers mentioned in such articles. Obviously these people are quite prominent in the field and are excellent candidates for your consideration.

Accountants

If your business is of any significant size, you will need the services of an accounting firm. The financial reporting requirements in Mexico are entirely different from those in the United States.

All the major U.S. accounting firms have offices in Mexico, but few are permitted to use their U.S. name. A call to any of their U.S. offices should set you up with the right person in Mexico.

If you do not need a huge multinational firm, select as you would select a lawyer: by personal referral. For tax, employment, or corporate financial questions, your accountant is your best bet. For general business guidance, an accountant's view might be too narrow, so find a specific consultant with expertise in your area of business.

Consultants

A knowledgeable consultant can be your most valuable resource when you are doing business with Mexico, whether the business involves importing a few thousand vases or establishing a major hotel complex. A number of international consulting firms all have their purpose, but your needs will relate specifically to Mexico, so select a firm with the same focus. The ideal adviser is bilingual and bicultural, at ease in both the United States and Mexico. Your best consultant will know how things really work rather than how the textbooks say they should. This person will be a full-time professional adviser to businesses associated with Mexico, a far cry from someone's brother-in-law living in Mexico who "knows everyone."

Your consultant will have extensive experience in Mexican business and trade. The firm will have many contacts, sources, and acquaintances in a variety of fields and government offices. It will know of additional opportunities in your area and be able to open doors you might never find on your own.

You are entering a country where success depends on who rather than what you know. Using an experienced consultant will save time and money. You will get to needed people and places without the newcomers' detours. Find the right consultant at the start of your business. Personal referrals are best, but again, interviewing is also a good idea. Whether you want research done, a few questions answered, a project completed, or a problem solved, begin with your consultant. As your requirements dictate, your consultant will know the best local professionals (attorneys, accountants, engineers, architects . . .) to handle your business.

COMMUNICATIONS

In the area of communications, Mexico is truly a Third World country. The phone system is outdated, overburdened, and completely inadequate to handle Mexico's needs. A substantial improvement program is ongoing, but until it is completed, you need to know the problems and alternatives. The government recognizes the need for efficient domestic and international communication. To be competitive worldwide, phone and mail service must be improved and streamlined. Privatizing Telmex has the phone system on the right course, but the mail service is not as promising. We explore alternatives below.

Phones

You will encounter certain problems with phone service in Mexico. Despite recent improvements, in some areas getting a phone line can still be a two-year process. Telephone numbers passed along with businesses and real estate are against the rules, but it is standard practice. Multiple phone lines are a rare luxury. In large businesses you often see desks with a number of single-line units. Call waiting and call holding are virtually unheard of in Mexico. Lines are often nonfunctional for days at a time, and directory assistance is a mass of confusion. But fear not because there are ways the knowledgeable communicate within Mexico and between our countries.

Express Services

DHL and Federal Express have replaced the mail system for our company. The 48 hours DHL takes is a vast improvement over possibly 48 days for normal mail service. UPS is up and coming in this market also, so compare rates and service.

Cellular Phones

Cellular phones are increasingly available in urban areas. In addition to being a growth opportunity for the 1990s, a cellular phone can be a lifesaver when your new business needs immediate communication. Although these phones are still somewhat expensive, many smaller businesses use them until permanent phone lines are installed.

FAX

The best answer to communication, particularly between Mexico and the United States, is the FAX machine. We have been saving thousands each month since installing these miraculous tools in our U.S. and Mexico offices. As we mentioned earlier in this chapter, each business communication must be preceded by social conversation. When you require only a quick piece of information, a $2 call can become a $50 issue. A FAX machine solves this problem.

Make sure you include the automatic redial feature on your FAX unit since getting a call through to Mexico can be an hour-long process. Yes, communications in Mexico are difficult, frustrating, and often expensive. Remember, however, that if you act now rather than later, Mexico offers thousands of fresh opportunities. A little expense and inconvenience now will put you light years ahead of your competition as Mexico's infrastructure improves. Unannounced area code changes and perplexing directory assistance are challenges to your inventiveness. Master the art of communication and find more opportunity.

TRANSPORTATION

From tourism to manufacturing, the transportation of goods and equipment is critical. The choice between ships, rail, trucks, and air depends on your individual needs. Most goods are transported in and out of Mexico by truck (4000 per day), so here we concentrate on this mode.

In arranging your transportation needs, balance the following factors:

Speed: Is what they promise realistic?

Safety: Are your goods insured by a reputable company?

Efficiency: Is the carrier familiar with the paperwork involved?

Economy: Are their rates competitive?

Experience: Does it speak for itself?

The average U.S. company probably cannot understand the range of all these factors. We are accustomed to fairly standard rates, maybe 10 percent up or down, and fairly dependable service. Let's consider Mexico first with a true story of what can go wrong and see how to make it go right.

Some years ago we were preparing our first shipment from Mexico City to San Francisco. We were "lucky" enough to find a major U.S. trucking company doing business with Mexico. We read the beautiful brochures with color pictures and promises of speed and efficiency. Like unknowing lambs dancing toward the slaughterhouse, we contracted for a 48-foot truck to transport our goods. After a week's delay, the truck arrived at our Mexico City warehouse for loading. Then off it drove. Two hours later we received a phone call from our associates in Mexico. The driver had been drunk, drove into a power pole, and knocked out the electricity for miles. The driver was in jail, the truck and everything confiscated! We called the major U.S. company; its response: "You hired him. We're not responsible for what happens in Mexico." What a nightmare.

A call to an ally in the government brought a quick release of the goods. Now, new truck, new driver, same company; the driver headed for the border and Mexican customs. He lost a day somewhere when he stopped en route to visit relatives. The truck finally arrived at the border. The so-called expert U.S. company had done the paperwork wrong (we now always do our own), so there were more days of delay.

When anything is even slightly out of the ordinary, Mexican customs conducts an intensive examination, in which the entire truck is unloaded at your expense and inspected in detail (at their convenience). If you have a commercial bond and do things regularly and correctly, this rarely happens. But we were novices in the hands of the trucking line from Hell, so customs did our intensive examination, leading to more paperwork, time, and money.

Our story continues to get worse! The expert trucking line told us that, to save time, they would bring the truck "in bond" to a San Francisco customs broker to avoid the wait at the border for U.S. customs. We said yes to their recommendation, which was a big mistake. Always use a U.S. broker at the border because such a broker is experienced, knows the local rules, and if something is wrong, can walk it through.

Our truck arrived at the trucking line's "regular" customs broker. The warehouse was actually a wholesale fish company; apparently the owner's brother sometimes did this brokering on the side. (Where the trucking line found these people we never found out.) After 21 days of constant screwups we got our truck.

We learned several lessons and paid for them dearly: this major U.S. company presented us with a bill triple what we now pay. "But you had the truck six weeks and look at all the extra work we did." Do not burn bridges. We paid and now advise our clients to use more efficient trucking lines.

We hope you learn the following from this experience:

Do not take transportation lightly.

Do not take competence for granted.

Look beyond brochures, and check experience.

Check with your consultant.

Ask for references and check them.

Shop for rates.

Always have a backup carrier.

Do not burn bridges.

Competence in the United States does not necessarily mean competence in Mexico.

After years we have developed fine relationships with economical and efficient trucking lines. We consider them a valuable resource for ourselves and anyone doing business with Mexico. It took time to find continually better rates and service, but it was well worth the effort.

Another transportation issue you need to consider in Mexico is the state of the roads. At this writing, road conditions are somewhere between bad and worse. Over the next few years things will get considerably better because 4000 kilometers of new toll highways and 7 international toll bridges are under construction. Mexico has 240,000 kilometers of highways, but only 95,000 are paved! Factor the cost and practicability of transportation into your business plan.

The port situation is similar. Recent privatizations have resulted in major modernizing now in progress. Mexico will have a number of world-class ports by the mid-1990s. About 80 percent of Mexico's transport needs are handled by truck, but these figures will change because imports and exports are increasing at a tremendous rate.

IMPROVEMENT

You're finally "doing it" in Mexico. Things are going well, and your venture is profitable. What now? Do you sit back and watch it all happen? No! In Mexico, as elsewhere, if you stagnate you will eventually fall behind.

We do not mean that you have not earned some relaxation. Nor do we suggest that you tear apart a coordinated venture only to begin again. Our suggestion is more casual: each week review one phase of your operation to see if there is room for improvement. This powerful yet surprisingly simple technique allows you to refine your operation continually. And our method keeps your subconscious focused and allows for an occasional flash of genius.

If you stay on top of new government regulations or incentives, new competitors, additional sources, alternative methods of transport, and the like, your venture will be in a constant state of progress. Consider the following situations.

Even the smallest business can benefit from a phase-by-phase analysis of its enterprise. A business importing Mexican goods from several sources should be looking at four factors.

New sources: Try someone new on a small scale from time to time. Improve your product line and have a backup supplier.

New and improved products from regular sources: Always look for cost-effective improvements to existing products, or for a whole new product line.

Transportation: Service and rates can vary over time with one company. Always be aware of what other transport concerns offer.

Customs broker: Service, rates, and personnel change here also. Investigate several to be certain the performance of yours is up to par. For the same services we were charged $1500 by one broker and $150 by another. Guess who we use now?

A maquila operation can also benefit from a consistent search for improvement. Many of the above concerns and especially the following should be reviewed from time to time.

New government incentives: The rules in Mexico change frequently, usually favoring the U.S. company. Be aware, anticipate change, and act.

New markets: This is important if you are in an expansion mode. Remember that you can get special exemptions to sell 50 percent of maquila-produced items in Mexico.

Spin-off products: Is there another similar product that can be added cost effectively to what you now offer?

Distribution: Your review should also look at the transportation issues.

In the tourism field there are countless sectors to review:

Government incentives and programs: Are you current on all the new programs for hotels, restaurants, and building in certain areas?

Opportunities in other areas: Might it be advantageous to open an additional location offering new investment opportunities?

Spin-off business: A restaurant near your hotel or condominiums on adjacent land might be an opportunity.

Vendors: Are all the suppliers to your part of the trade the best for your situation? Are you getting the most for your money? Investigate constantly and improve your profit.

As you can see, it is important to be on the lookout for ways to refine your enterprise. Staying up-to-date can only enhance your position. In Mexico particularly, things change at a startling pace. Increase your awareness.

Throughout your search for improvement, remember the importance of loyalty. Be loyal to your suppliers even at a small additional cost. The time to change is when they are disloyal to you. If your ally in one company moves to another, consider following that person. Policies or quality changes in your suppliers' organizations may also cause you to consider a change.

You should be proud that you have developed a profitable venture in Mexico. Your search for improvement should be automatic and enjoyable. Our phase-by-phase analysis should help you focus on certain areas and make progress more efficient. Consider also the possibility of bringing in a third-party expert for a fresh outlook on the areas of your business. New opportunities or areas for improvement you have not considered often exist.

6

ELEVEN PITFALLS YOU CAN AVOID

—

Here we show you how to save time, money, and no small amount of consternation. Thousands of U.S. and Canadian businesses have already taken the plunge and expanded into Mexico. Some 200 businesspeople have shared their experiences with us. Their business interests range from technology to agriculture, from textiles to transportation, but their stories all have common threads running through them. At its inception, each commercial concern made choices, decisions, and plans. What appeared correct then sometimes later proved erroneous and costly. But the concerns learned from their experiences, and most went on to substantial success.

In interviewing these business leaders, we found common mistakes many made when they first started in Mexico. Eleven of these mistakes showed up so often that we want to warn you about these pitfalls. In this chapter we look at how to identify them, how to avoid making the same mistakes yourself, and how to best turn these possible pitfalls into opportunities for jumping ahead of your competition. Learn from the mistakes of others and revise your plans and expectations accordingly.

OVERCOMING THE MAÑANA SYNDROME

We studied the mañana syndrome in Chapter 2. Most Mexicans move at their own pace. Fighting against this pace will leave you frustrated, but riding it with subtle steering and guidance will make you a master of Mexican trade. Let's discuss how to read between the lines, solve problems by anticipation, follow up, use diplomacy to soothe fragile egos while applying real-life solutions, and distinguish between the mañana syndrome and outright lying.

When a Mexican supplier promises you a specific date, he honestly intends to perform as agreed. But two things can go wrong.

Suppliers Want You to Be Happy

First, understand that your supplier or his workers truly want you to be happy, and not just to keep your business. They simply are nice people who hate stress. So they immediately determine what will make you happy as they see it. For example, to your query about a shipment, they may reply, "Your shipment went out yesterday, Senora." You are happy to hear this, and the worker intends to send the promised shipment immediately after lunch. But often something comes up after lunch, so the goods stay where they are for a few days. We cover the solution shortly, but now let's look at a second mañana pitfall.

Implied Clause in Every Contract

You must be aware of the existence in every contract with a supplier in Mexico that an implied clause considers delays caused by important events perfectly acceptable. This is not a written law, but everyone in Mexico acknowledges its existence. Here is an example of how it works. Recently we were told that a container load of furniture would take 2 weeks to manufacture and prepare for shipping. We had been through this situation before, so we knew that the delivery time would be at least 30 days. For the first week following the order, production would be normal. But coming up was Semana Santa (Easter Week). The first two days of the second week would be normal, but the rest of the week's production would be lost as everyone prepared for this most important of all weeks. During the third week, the actual Easter week, no business would occur in Mexico; presumably both contracting parties would know that these 7 days would not be included. The fourth week, the workers would be understandably slow after a week-long fiesta. We all realized at the time of contracting that the goods would be ready in 30 days. In fact, they were indeed ready then, and both parties agreed that the contract was carried out in a timely fashion.

"Important events" in the unwritten clause of a Mexican contract include national holidays, state holidays, citywide celebrations, marriages, deaths, births, phone or electrical outages, and natural disasters. Other events will arise as you conduct business; if you are a

master of Mexican business, you will recall this section
and smile.

Solutions

The solutions to both types of "problems" are anticipation, follow-up, and diplomacy. First, anticipate the
mañana syndrome in its various guises. Question the
response "Your shipment left our factory Tuesday."
Then follow up to make sure things are as promised:
make a quick call to the next delivery point (or maybe
your customs broker) to see if the goods arrived. Now use
your diplomacy. Call the supplier, to show you are on
top of the matter. "I just called the customs broker. The
truck hasn't arrived yet. You're probably better at this
than I am. Perhaps you could trace the shipment?"
Pause for a moment. "I'll call back in two hours to see
what you have found out" (this will be more follow-up).

Our clients are always amazed at how we reduce
shipping time by weeks using this technique. If you use
it every time, your suppliers will expect the follow-up
and give you better service to avoid the trouble. Always,
however, consider the ego of the person involved and
offer your "help" in the proper manner.

This delicate presentation is also an issue when
dealing with another aspect of the mañana syndrome.
"It's impossible" often means "I see no way to do this
in the time I have with the effort I am willing to ex-
pend." To succeed in Mexico, your attitude should be
that "impossible" simply means a little more work than
"possible."

Here is an example. Say it is Friday afternoon, 4:30.
If your shipment does not clear customs tonight, the

paperwork will not even be looked at until Monday afternoon. You hear the words "It's impossible" and remember our lesson. It is standard practice that for a nominal fee (regulated by statute), the customs inspector will stay a couple of extra hours. You arrange for this, but now you must inform your customs broker about the situation without offending him. Explain that only with his guidance were you able to create this miracle. This way you avoid future resentment and possibly create an ally. Make certain the broker feels part of the solution and that you truly appreciate his special assistance. Feed his ego, not yours, and profit.

Not often, but often enough so you need to be aware of it, people take the mañana syndrome a step too far. For example, the shipment your supplier claims went out Tuesday has not even been produced yet. This is outright laziness and lying, not an amusing cultural idiosyncrasy. Depending on the immediacy of your need, you either get out of the agreement diplomatically and find another supplier, or you finesse the actual production without calling the supplier a liar. Remember, even in this sort of situation, diplomacy is the key. Burn no bridges. Accept occasional frustration and enjoy your profits.

There are countless variations of the mañana syndrome and ways it will affect your business. Consider initially retaining a professional to spot weak areas so you might anticipate them and save time. Within a year or sooner, with experience and/or guidance, anticipation, follow-up, and diplomacy will become second nature to you. Your U.S. associates will be astounded at the efficiency of your Mexican operation. Your response will be, "I just work with terrific people." And your Mexican associates will be proud of having created so many miracles to help you succeed.

TRAPS FOR THE UNWARY

You are going to Mexico, where most people seem friendly and life appears good. Business situations seem more relaxed. Social activity from fiestas to lunching fills your itinerary. Go ahead, enjoy this great way of doing business, but do not let your guard down. Avoid the following traps.

Underestimating

Do not underestimate the Mexican people. Some businesspeople think that everything is the same in Mexico as it is in the United States, but it is not. Do not be condescending. Those who equate a person's accent with stupidity overlook the fact that this person is at least bilingual. Similarly, do not misconstrue silence as a failure to understand; in negotiations you will notice that the person who says the least gets the most. Avoid these traps. Be prepared to accept that those with whom you are dealing may be more experienced, educated, and/or worldly than yourself.

Falsifying Customs Paperwork

Much of the duty charged is based on the invoices you provide. Even if your supplier swears that "It's done all the time," do not think that you will deceive either U.S. or Mexican customs. The agents are pretty sharp and have seen it all. A ploy to save a little money might work once, but you are jeopardizing your entire venture and possibly your freedom. If you get caught using false invoices, your bond will be revoked, and you may lose all import/export privileges.

Get-Rich-Quick Schemes

Do not be a yokel and fall for get-rich-quick schemes simply because you are in another country. Mexico has countless variations of these scams, many sounding plausible to the uninitiated. Three rules should govern your conduct:

- Check out your alliances.
- If it is too good to be true, even in Mexico, it is not true.
- Whenever money is involved, you should always control it as much as possible. Always minimize risk.

Be careful. Any time you are about to put your signature on something or transfer funds, exercise extreme caution. Ask yourself, "Am I being stupid?" This question will save you money, time, and self-respect. If you are about to transfer your retirement savings to someone you met last week so you can get in on the ground floor of a worm farm in Baja, think "Will I really lose this opportunity if the money isn't transferred by 4 o'clock?"

"Why doesn't this guy have a phone?" Do not leave your
common sense at the border.

Drugs

Of course you know you should avoid drugs personally,
but what about in your business dealings? Whenever
merchandise crosses the border, there is a chance someone has included a secret package of drugs. If at all possible, ship in sealed trucks and containers. Without this
and other precautions you might find yourself a suspect
in a drug-smuggling case. Morally and legally you have
a duty to guard against concealed shipments of drugs.
Mexican jails are quite unpleasant, and bail is nonexistent.

Trademark or Copyright Infringement

In the more tawdry end of business you hear "We'll
knock 'em off in Mexico." Translated, this means that
the person intends to circumvent another person's possibly protected rights by producing a similar, possibly
mislabeled, product in Mexico. Particularly sleazy operators use a few loopholes to do this very thing. We
strongly advise against this practice for two reasons.
First, it is morally reprehensible. Why consider something illegal when there are so many legitimate opportunities? Second, recent new laws and regulations in
Mexico have put some serious teeth into copyright and
trademark infringement penalties. The Mexican author-
ities are looking for someone to make an example of, so

a flashy, high-rolling gringo knocking off Levis or Reeboks would be a favorite case to prosecute.

Common Sense

Of all the rules to follow, the most important ones are those of common sense, conscience, and good business. Respect your associates and do the right thing. Look before you leap and avoid unnecessary hazards.

ANALYZING YOUR COMPETITION

You have outlined your business plan, and everything seems ready to go. A possible pitfall easy to avoid at this stage is the competition. Opportunities in Mexico are substantial, and the country is huge, but do not let these factors lull you into a false sense of security. Sound business planning is still necessary; checking out the competition is mandatory.

First, research the industry in general, identifying the players in your field in both the United States and Mexico. Next, investigate individual companies. Public records and library materials are useful background information, but another crucial step is a visit to these businesses. Although some companies will rebuff your efforts even if you approach them as a potential customer, others will be helpful. We have found that the most successful organizations are those quite open to sharing basic information. Those barely hanging on are the most secretive. Look, ask questions, and make alliances for possible joint ventures later. These people have been where you are going, and their insights can be invaluable, so pay attention.

The third step is analyzing your competition from a different perspective. Approach your potential customers at this stage, acquiring information. Find key people and ask if they are being served well by your future competitors. Might your slightly different service, product, or price seem attractive to them? Get information, make alliances for the future, and learn. The people you meet during this analysis can be candidates for managerial positions in your company later. Certainly you will not broach this subject during a fact-finding tour, but keep it in mind.

If you are too busy to do the groundwork for competition analysis, hire a professional to do it for you. Knowledge of the marketplace is too important to be left to chance. Time and money invested at this stage might well be the difference between dismal failure and astounding success. Do not skimp.

As you analyze your competition, keep the following five questions in mind:

1. Are they operating in Mexico already?

2. What problems have they encountered?

3. What opportunities have they found?

4. Can you compete in price, service, or quality?

5. What do potential customers want?

By analyzing your competition, you can avoid pitfalls and anticipate problems. Learn from their mistakes and their victories. Invest whatever it takes to know your competition. The information is invaluable and necessary for you to maximize your profits.

Partnerships Versus
Other Alternatives

With the exception of a few industries, you no longer legally need a Mexican partner to do business in Mexico. Now the choice is yours. Let's consider the pros and cons of partnerships and, if you do decide on a partnership, to protect your investment, the important safeguards. If a partnership is not for you, consider the alternatives that might be better in certain situations.

A partnership has been described as an agreement wherein you have an apple on your head and your partner has a bow and arrow. And when international borders are involved, a partnership is like handing your partner a blindfold before he shoots. For one reason or another, partnerships rarely last long. And Mexico has an inefficient legal system that often protects a local over a U.S. business, so consider this handicap before signing a partnership agreement.

Sometimes a partnership is ideal. When one party has what the other needs and vice versa, such an arrangement can work. Particularly when you are in a foreign country, your partner might have knowledge of great value to you. Subject to the safeguards we now discuss, the most profitable way to use this expertise might be a partnership.

Safeguards

If you are considering a partnership, take into account the safeguards. First, ask yourself if your proposed partners are too eager. Unfortunately, in Mexico, as elsewhere, people are wanting to form an instant "partnership" and take your money. Be careful. Check references and work by personal referral.

Have Mexican and U.S. lawyers draft an agreement responding to specific issues in Mexican law. A paragraph in this accord should provide for any disagreements to be resolved in U.S. courts under U.S. law. Check with your lawyer. This agreement should set out each party's specific rights and duties, to avoid misunderstandings later. When a partnership makes too much money or begins to operate at a loss, disagreements arise, and they can increase when laws and customs are different between the countries. Finally, the ultimate safeguard: regardless of the expense or inconvenience, *you* should always directly control the money.

Associations

Consider an association, whereby you have one or a number of associates, each with a different area of expertise. You join forces only when you need that particular knowledge; you terminate your association on completion of that phase of your project. Each member will profit according to personal contribution. An association does not last long, and everyone remains friends. We have quite a number of associates in Mexico, each having special knowledge and talents. We can therefore provide a variety of consulting services because we have different experts available for our clients' unique requirements. Associations are a loose, independent-contractor arrangement and offer more flexibility than a partnership.

Joint Ventures

A joint venture is more formal than an association but not as encompassing as a partnership. It is an agreement to accomplish one limited goal, each party's rights being limited to that one achievement. For example, a written agreement may provide that one party gets the funding and the other party builds some apartments. Upon sale of the apartments, the agreement is terminated and the profits are disbursed. If your goals are easily definable and limited in scope, a joint venture will limit your exposure and maximize your profits.

Licensing Agreements

For businesses with a definite name/marketing identity in Mexico, licensing agreements are ideal. Chains of U.S. restaurants and apparel, retailing, and other industries have been active in this area. The company's name and method of operation are offered to a Mexican company that in turn opens, owns, and manages the company in Mexico. The sale of licensing rights is a big business between the United States and Mexico. The legal issues are complex, so be certain to retain an attorney to handle specific details.

We have been fortunate in our own experiences with partnerships in Mexico. They have been textbook studies in trust, integrity, and profit. We also have personally been involved in all three alternatives to a partnership and have found each one ideal depending on the situation. These formalized alliances can be the key to your success as long as you use professionals and common sense to determine what might be right for your business. Do it right and avoid pitfalls later.

QUALITY REVIEW AND CONTROL

Quality control is important when doing business anywhere, and Mexico is no exception. Do not fall victim to the "out of sight, out of mind" pitfall. Most likely you will be based in the United States while your business continues in Mexico. Avoid problems and be vigilant concerning the quality of your product or service.

Manufacturing

In manufacturing you can create a truly superior product cost-effectively. Although Mexico historically has the reputation of mediocre quality, remember the Made in Japan label of post-World War II. Japan now has the reputation for high quality, and Mexico, in some areas, is doing even better. Your concern for excellence will benefit Mexico as well as your bottom line. Whether you are manufacturing as a maquila or your product is being produced under a licensing agreement, you should send in your own quality control team, as companies such as Gucci, General Motors, and Mcdonald's do. The practice is so prevalent that the labor laws include specific exemptions for quality control personnel.

Import/Export

The import/export arena is another field where you must review quality. Obviously you have less control here than in your own manufacturing unit, but there are ways to safeguard your product. Contracts should contain the minimum specifications you will accept. Sign off on each phase of production to avoid an insurmountable problem upon completion. Remember, when your supplier is producing beyond capacity, quality suffers. For quality and other reasons it is better for you to have two or three suppliers. Finally, if 5 percent or less of goods received from an ongoing supplier is unacceptable, do not charge back for the goods the first time. Instead, point out the problem, suggesting better attention next time. Quite possibly the supplier did its best or was laboring under a misunderstanding. In either event, take the small loss this one time as a cost of goodwill.

Restaurants and Hotels

Quality is especially important for restaurants, hotels, and other tourist facilities. Although these organizations are frequently established through licensing agreements with Mexican companies or individuals, your name is still on them. Your original contract should provide specifically for quality standards in every arena. Go to the additional expense of having your staff on site, and take the extra time to visit them personally. Your worldwide reputation is affected by the quality of service your customers receive in Mexico.

Product and service integrity are the secrets to success for many businesses. Your constant attention to these matters will reap rich rewards. Insist on strict adherence to your standards, even if additional expense for training and supervising workers is involved. Show pride in your product and you will benefit by personnel who care about quality. One auto manufacturer, with a strict quality control program, is now turning out cars of such quality that they have canceled plans to add robotics at their plant; the Mexican workers are more precise!

Anticipate about one year of intense quality supervision and refinement. Within that year, everyone will learn what is expected of them, the inept will be weeded out, and systems for assuring continuous quality can be put in place. Once your standards are established and the work force trimmed, superior production will be the norm.

STOCK AND PERMIT SCAMS

Despite its proximity to us, Mexico is truly a foreign country to most U.S. citizens. The clever scam artist uses this cloak of mystery as a tool to fleece unknowing investors and businesspeople. There are countless ways money is bilked from the unsuspecting in Mexico, but four methods are sufficiently common to warrant specific warnings: two types of securities fraud and two fairly standard permit deceptions. Unfortunately, the swindlers perpetrating these hoaxes are often successful. International borders protect them, and even if the crooks are found, enforcement of your rights is a difficult and time-consuming process, so be forewarned.

Stock Scams

The first stock scam is outright forgery. Expensively printed stock certificates (or other security instruments such as bonds) are offered. Everyone has been reading about the huge returns on Mexican stocks, and who wouldn't want to get in on the next Telmex? In the United States, law enforcement officials recently broke up a multimillion dollar Mexican bond forgery ring on the East Coast. Unhappily, many more frauds go unprosecuted. You are on your own, so watch out. The three signs to look for are:

1. The deal is always "Once in a lifetime."

2. You just recently met the person presenting the offer (although he looks and sounds good, he seems like your very best friend).

3. There is always some severe time pressure, often involving the immediate wire transfer of funds. Your questions are answered in such a manner that you feel foolish asking more: "Sure it is Saturday, but we must do this before the big announcement Monday morning at the exchange! Maybe we should just leave you out of this one."

The second, more substantial con involves the use of shell corporations in Mexico. Anyone can put together an apparently substantial business in Mexico. Beautiful letterhead ($50) with offices listed worldwide—most people do not call the Trinidad or Lisbon phone numbers to confirm that they exist—and just the Mexico City office (maybe a $40 per month apartment) are all that are necessary. The Finance Ministry will even confirm the corporation's existence. Whatever the "corporation" is offering, consider two cautions. First, never release any funds without independent (not the references being provided) verification that the deal is solid.

Second, always look at the substance of the transaction, not simply the form. For example, in a land swindle, the con artists have aerial photographs, mineral studies, architect's drawings, letters from the mayor, and much more in a really well-presented package. But who has the title to the land, and where is the proof? Consider these and the recommended cautions in the previous discussion in any corporate transaction you enter. Never hesitate to go to Mexico to check out the deal. If you are talking about a substantial investment, $400 for plane tickets is pretty inexpensive insurance.

Permit Fraud

Many U.S. businesspersons are regularly hoodwinked about the acquisition and granting of permits. Uninformed people, new to Mexico, are particularly at risk in these situations. Until 10 years ago, a significant amount of corruption in the area of permits existed in Mexico. Many people still use that outdated information and are therefore particularly gullible to permit hoaxes.

The first standard permit deception involves telling you that a permit is needed when there is no such requirement. This fraud is easy to spot, but businesspeople fall for it every day. Your lawyer knows what permits are needed, so your ultimate safeguard is to deal strictly through him or her. A sure sign of permit fraud is the demand for cash only. Also, the swindler always comes to your office (he has no phone number to back him up), and when you hesitate or suggest checking on him, he utters some fairly dire threats.

The second and somewhat more sophisticated permit ruse can occur when you really need a permit for something. Your lawyer has told you that it may take quite some time. Along comes a particularly likable fellow who "has a cousin in that exact department." Using your outdated knowledge of the way things work in Mexico, you stupidly part with a significant amount of cash for the fellow to smooth the permit process. This sort of person will come back again and again: "Just one more guy needs to get his bonus and it will be approved." "These people are thieves; it's a good thing you have me helping you or it would cost many thousands more."

We hope that these warnings will be unnecessary and that you will take along your common sense to Mexico. Also, do not think that we are slamming Mexico by pointing out these frauds. Scams, scandals, and scoundrels thrive in every country. When you deal internationally, these scams sometimes work because there is more that visiting businesspeople do not know, and that lack of knowledge is used against them. Remember: Do not hurry, check independent references, look at form and substance, and do not be cheap—go to Mexico to check out any transaction for yourself.

SELECTING A CUSTOMS BROKER

When properly selected, your customs broker can be a valuable business tool. Carelessly chosen, that person can throw you into one pitfall from which your business might never recover. Here we consider what customs brokers do and the benefits they offer. You will learn how to make the best choice, how to handle the money, and consider etiquette in this area. Basically, here is an overview of what happens to goods crossing the border from Mexico:

Goods → Mexican customs broker → Mexican customs →
  U.S. customs broker → U.S. customs to you

(The converse is true for goods entering Mexico.)

Your goods arrive with the appropriate documents at your Mexican customs broker, who fills out the forms and acts as your liaison with Mexican customs, handles any questions and any required follow-up, and coordinates timing with the Mexican customs inspector. Next, your goods pass through to your U.S. customs broker, who repeats the process. Finally, the shipment is released from U.S. customs to your carrier.

A word on customs employees. Customs in both the United States and Mexico are government agencies and should be treated as such. There are no mysteries and few vendettas. The inspectors simply want to make sure you are doing things correctly and paying the appropriate fees and duty. All information from your crossing goes into customs' computers for future reference. The inspectors are not there to act as an information service, although they can be quite helpful. Their job is easier when everything is done right in advance. They appreciate the work of a well-selected customs broker. Naturally, the reverse is also true. If you use a sloppy broker, customs will vent their wrath on you and your shipment. Treat these people with the respect they deserve. Make sure certain things are done right so your shipment will go smoothly.

Although some people believe they do not need a customs broker, you do. As in other fields, you should stick to what you do best and leave the rest to experts. A good customs broker provides five benefits:

1. He is familiar with all types of paperwork: forms, documents, visas, exemptions, and so on.

2. He is familiar with the system.

3. He is aware of any changes in the system and rules as they occur, e.g., the new rule that all upholstered furniture must be certified fire-resistant.

4. He is close by and can act when customs is ready; you do not have to hire someone to sit 24 hours a day and wait.

5. He is bonded and regulated, so you can be confident of his basic honesty.

Customs brokers can prove invaluable in countless ways as your relationship continues. Once you have found a good one, stay loyal and make an alliance.

The selection process is a little difficult. The U.S. customs booklet lists some of the larger brokers (note that we are not saying "better"), but we know from personal experience that this is not the best way to choose one. Without a personal referral you are treading on dangerous ground. Always ask your attorney or consultant for suggestions about who might best meet your company's needs. Check references, and make certain the broker's bond is current. Once you have an ongoing relationship, consider visiting the broker, unannounced, at some time when you have a shipment crossing.

Brokers provide a wide variety of services, from document preparation to storage or marking. Your fees will vary depending on the services you require. Some brokers make payments on your behalf and bill you later. In such situations, make sure the payments were indeed made. We learned this the hard way when our first customs broker failed to pay some government fees, although we had paid him. Severe consequences await those who do not pay governments. Beyond the services, fees also vary among different brokers. Some will charge you more simply because you do not know better. The more responsible brokers are quite fair and want your business for the long run.

When you find a good customs broker, stay loyal and do not circumvent the broker's actions, even if doing so costs a little more, because charges will prove minimal. The broker is your representative—use him accordingly. Calling customs directly when you have a customs broker is a definite breach of etiquette. Pursue this course only in the most severe circumstances.

From outside appearances there is little difference between a pitfall and a gold mine. Your customs broker can be either. Check with their other clients, use personal referral where possible, and spare no effort in proper selection. Just sounding good on the phone is not enough; look for substantive proof that the broker provides excellent service at a reasonable price.

OUTDATED INFORMATION

In any country you must keep up to date in business. This adage is even more important if you are doing business with Mexico. Great changes have taken place in Mexican business, including the overall economic climate, practices, rules, and taxes. First we look at the situations where up-to-date information is critical and then list sources for data necessary to keep your operation running smoothly.

One situation we consistently see is a business that researched Mexico's opportunities 2, 5, or even 10 years ago. The business came up against prohibitions that are no longer in effect. Other businesses found that under the rules of that time, there was no cost-effective way to accomplish their goals, so they then closed their minds to Mexico. These very same people are now amazed to hear of the sweeping changes, such as effective ownership of coastal lands available to U.S. citizens and businesses and a program that did not work five years ago for a textile firm being effective now.

All too often we see more serious situations. For example, a business currently trading in Mexico or about to begin a project is operating on out-of-date information. It has not kept up. Its business plan does not take into account the possible effects of the North American Free Trade Agreement and its phase-in period, environmental regulations, changes in labor rules, phaseout of tariffs, and the effect of those changes on its competition. These businesspeople are in a dangerous position. They need to have new information to keep their competitive edge. Perhaps they could do business more profitably under new programs or rules. Up-to-date information is a high priority for international business.

Seemingly minor rules change without receiving much attention. If one such regulation affects you, you need to know about it. Your failure to keep up to date on the rules influencing your industry might stop an important shipment, leave a project incomplete, or put you in some other grave position.

There are solutions to these issues. Government

programs are presently being instituted for several areas of business. In the tourism, agriculture, and maquiladora sectors, where information has been conflicting, these new programs are intended to provide current and consistent information to interested parties. Other reports can bring you up to date on taxes and customs.

Several alternative methods for keeping up to date are in their infancy. Newsletters and new business publications can bring you constant news of changes in your industry. Do not forget the American Chamber of Commerce in Mexico. Their mission, to promote trade and information, is the key to your project. Many other sources of current information are in our Resource Guide.

Finally, remember to use your professionals. Your attorney, accountant, and consultant are involved in many aspects of business every day. They not only keep current on new rules but are in a position to anticipate changes in various industries.

The lesson here is to not rely on out-of-date information. Fundamental changes are quickly taking place in United States/Mexico trade. Whether you are just doing initial research or beginning a project, or even if you are already established, you must keep up to date. Use the many ways to improve your position and avoid pitfalls. There's an information boom in Mexican business. Take advantage of this opportunity.

ADVANCE PAYMENTS

A small- to medium-sized company particularly will encounter the issue of advance payments when sourcing its products in Mexico. It will be asked to pay before receiving the goods or services. Here we cover why this is to be expected and how to turn a potential pitfall into a business tool.

Advance payments for huge, multinational companies contracting with Mexican megacompanies are handled much the same as in the United States. No one ever really sees the money because it is handled as debits, credits, letters of credit, and the like between banks and accountants. Neither party fears the other's ability to pay or produce.

For a small- to medium-size business on either side of the trade, advance payments are a necessity for several reasons. One reason is the difficulty of enforcing a contract between a Mexican and U.S. company. Receiving a deposit protects the providing concern against loss. Another reason is that an advance payment allows a small company to obtain required materials. Subject to the safeguards we discuss below, you can go ahead and provide a deposit, but never advance payment in full. Before determining the size of deposit, consider which gets the fastest service:

1. A company with no deposit and a reputation for slow payment.

2. A company that made a 50 percent advance payment, the balance COD or net 30.

3. A company that paid the full amount prior to production.

Selection 3 might be the correct response in the United States, but selection 2 is the correct one in Mexico. Remember the mañana syndrome. After protecting yourself, negotiate for a deposit arrangement. But do watch quality. In hurrying the final portion of your order, quality may suffer. Your original agreement should provide for charge-backs if production is not up to standards. An alternative is signing off at each stage and making progress payments. Adapt this principle to your business.

Here is how to minimize the possibility of losing your deposits:

1. Check the personal reputation of the person with whom you are negotiating.

2. Use your alliances to inquire about the business' reputation.

3. Ask for verifiable trade references.

4. Make inquiries about the concern's solvency.

5. Enlist the resources of a professional if you are unable to complete steps 1 to 4.

6. Set up a local banking relationship. Bankers, when allies, are a wealth of financial information and exceedingly cautious.

Thus, you can minimize the risk of loss on advance payments. You can use the deposit and amounts due to your advantage. Be cautious, but at all times present your caution within the bounds of business etiquette.

GRINGO GO HOME

We hope you will never encounter the "gringo go home" attitude, which is unpleasant and potentially fatal to your business. Learn to avoid the pitfalls.

What is a gringo anyway? Why would Mexicans want them to go home? The answer is in the history of Mexico. As we discussed in Chapter 2, the United States invaded Mexico at one time. The green-uniformed U.S. soldiers were so pushy and impolite that everywhere were heard shouts of "Green coats go home!" Say this phrase quickly and with a Spanish accent and out comes "Gringo go home!" As a result of the invasion, the U.S. arguably snatched away half of Mexico's country (Texas, California, Arizona, and New Mexico), so understandably even today there is an inherent mistrust of the gringo.

The Mexicans are an understanding people, tolerating our cultural ineptitude and welcoming us despite our historical piracy. However, several practices will incur their displeasure. First, no one appreciates a condescending attitude. The Mexicans are sensitive to this issue because their history is replete with rulers trying to subjugate them. Allow for cultural differences. We are certainly no better than they are and vice versa. Condescension will close doors in a hurry.

Second, do not be an ugly American. Follow the rules of business and social etiquette. Respect is more important than currency in Mexico (and perhaps more valuable). If you "get no respect," you probably did not give it and therefore are worthy of none. Ugly American equals gringo equals go home. Be respectful and earn your place in Mexico.

A third way to infuriate a Mexican businessperson is to insensitively cast aside Mexican business practices and force your own ideas in their place. Business practices in the United States are much different from those in Mexico, many of which are founded in cultural traditions of historical and social importance. There is a flow to Mexican business. Steer your business along with the flow. Do not try to swim upstream or you will become a hated gringo.

Finally, do not be a carpetbagger. Show concern for Mexico's people and ecology. Mexico is opening its doors to long-term opportunities for you. Shove your way in and ignore local customs at your peril.

Any of these four mistakes will stir up old prejudices. The welcome mat will be withdrawn, and you will not be given a second chance. Come as a neighbor and show respect. You will be welcomed, and all of Mexico will be open.

UNREALISTIC EXPECTATIONS

As a new entry into Mexican business, you must be a realist. Mexico is truly an economic horn of plenty that might dazzle you with potential profits. However, do not let your bedazzlement lead you toward the serious pitfall of unrealistic expectations. Beyond doubt, Mexico's businesses will continue to strengthen as international trade and investment grow dramatically. Please note, however, that such a national undertaking involving significant worldwide consequences cannot occur without a hitch or twist of some type. The election of an unlikely candidate or some other world event might affect the course Mexico follows. Mexico's growth, stability, and entrance into the world market are inevitable. For your own safety, and to grasp new opportunities as they arise, keep an eye on world and Mexican political/economic events. You could turn a potential pitfall into a gold mine.

Also, do not assume that everything "can be had" in Mexico for pennies on the dollar. True, lowered labor costs and Mexico's abundant raw materials often lead to savings in purchases and production sometimes 75 percent below U.S. costs. But the Mexican workers are people and citizens, not slaves, so do not enter into business or trade anticipating taking advantage of Mexico and its people. You may safely forecast significant savings in many areas of business without economic pillaging. Invest in Mexico's growth and profit along with the country. Accept and enjoy the opportunities offered to you. Do not be greedy.

Temper expectations with realism. Regardless of how smart or lucky you are, do not count on things going right the first time, which rarely happens even in the comparatively sophisticated U.S. business world. With proper planning and advice, you may forecast a profitable venture from the outset. Anticipate, however, that unforeseeable things will go wrong initially. Your lowered costs may keep you profitable at this initial stage, but the large profits come later. Armed with new facts about what can go wrong, make changes in your operation so it will function more profitably and smoothly. But, in a culture and environment new to you, additional problems will arise, so count on continuous fine-tuning. Your profits will rise and stabilize as your experience increases. Anticipate these initial problems and incorporate the additional time and expense into your plans. Avoid frustration and consider that you are paying for education.

Do not expect things to be like they are in the United States. You should anticipate necessary adjustments to find your place in Mexico's business world. You will not get rich quickly, however, because more money does not necessarily solve every problem. Unrealistic expectations can cloud your judgment. Avoid them, be a realist, enjoy, and learn from the unexpected. Be prepared to adapt and grow.

7

EMERGING AREAS
OF OPPORTUNITY

FRANCHISING

Until 1989, franchising in Mexico was very difficult.
All franchises had to be approved by the Technology
Transfer Bureau, a subsidiary of the Ministry of Commerce. This nightmare bureaucracy reflected Mexico's
economic nationalism of the time. The primary concern
was that U.S. companies would franchise into Mexico
and royalty payments would go from Mexican franchises
to U.S. companies; that is, much needed capital would
leave the country. A few franchises went through the
paper jungle and gained approvals after about two years.
Holiday Inn, Kentucky Fried Chicken, and McDonalds
were the pioneers that suffered from the red tape of earlier years.

As with the rest of Mexico's economy, new rules favor franchise investment in the New Mexico. The government's position now is that royalties are a small price to pay for the immediate investment in Mexico, jobs, and know-how. The trend is toward less regulation. Approval processes have been streamlined to 45 days, government-imposed maximums on royalty rates no longer exist, and new laws allow protection of concepts and know-how. The Commerce Ministry is hoping that Mexican businesses will (1) learn from U.S. firms and spread that knowledge to other service industries and (2) show how local businesses can be franchised to enter the U.S. and Canadian markets, for example, El Pollo Loco, which began in Mazatlan.

Government is pushing the franchise concept, but other factors make these opportunities even more inviting. First, Mexico City, Guadalajara, Monterrey, and some border areas are the population centers, with a very high concentration of people, making a dream market for franchises. Second, half the population is under 20, a potential younger market of people who are brand-loyal for things American. Third, more than 30 million of Mexico's near-100 million population are now able to afford the products that franchises are offering.

Franchises are entering Mexico at a record rate; Mail Boxes Etc., Subway, Domino's Pizza, Chili's Hamburgers, Blockbuster Video, Athlete's Foot, and Kwik Kopy have all been very well received. Real estate, business services, and weight control are other fields just now entering this lucrative market. Taco Bell is even opening quite a number of outlets! If you have a franchise or a franchisable concept, Mexico is the new market. Government support, a huge demand, and concentrated population centers all ensure your success.

INVESTMENT BANKING

We read about the privatizations, mergers, acquisitions, new public offerings, and the like. Billions of investment dollars are created seemingly from nowhere. Where does the money come from? Who profits from this capital movement? Just what amount of resources (money) are involved? Who are the players? What are the opportunities?

In 1990, close to $2 billion in foreign funds were invested in Mexico via capital investment. The 1991 figures were more than $6 billion. Privatizations and new public offerings created much of this activity. Investors outside Mexico believe in the country's stability and future growth. These investors will reap good returns over the long run, but huge profits are being made as we speak. The foreign intermediaries for these capital accessing ventures are earning fees from 3 to 6 percent of the sales price, that is, hundreds of millions of dollars.

About 10 international firms are making the lion's share of these profits, but other firms are entering the field. The U.S.-based Citibank, Salomon Brothers, Bear Stearns, and Goldman Sachs are the investment banking leaders. Known for their stability and reputations for success in global capital markets, these companies have been instrumental in putting together the billion-dollar deals that brought to Mexico the foreign capital necessary for creating its economic miracle.

There is not much left to be privatized, so where is the opportunity for the future? Private industry rather than government. Mergers and acquisitions will be most active as the larger Mexican companies position themselves to be more globally competitive. With phased-in

lifting of restrictions on foreign investment in the country, the Mexican players are operating within a limited
time frame. Streamline and join forces or perish in the
face of international competition is the rule of the day.

New public offerings of smaller companies—$100
million in annual revenues—will occur more and more
often as privately held companies go public and smaller
companies merge into multiservice industries. These
transactions will be greater in number, with smaller capital requirements, so the market awaits a new level of
intermediaries. After all, 6 percent of $100 million is still
a fee worth pursuing. The giant businesses may consider
these deals too small, which means less competition for
those entering this area of capital markets.

The upcoming new exchange in Mexico will provide a capital market for small and emerging companies
($3 million to $30 million). The setup will be quite similar to our NASDAQ. Smaller, aggressive commercial
banks, financial service companies, and consulting firms
are the likely candidates for success in this newly emerging opportunity.

PREFABRICATED/OTHER
LOW-COST HOUSING

Mexico has a serious need for additional very low-cost
housing. With the new economy, many families will no
longer need to live in virtual homelessness. The industrial areas particularly have inadequate civilized housing
for the rapidly growing work force. The employers are
interested in providing adequate shelter for their

workers, and the employees who are now making a bit more in wages want to provide a better home for their families.

Guadiana, headquartered in Chihuahua, has been the major player in prefab housing to date. The company is doing very well, but others are entering this virtually unlimited field. Other prefab companies are entering the Mexican market, while U.S. homebuilders are investigating possibilities in the maquiladora areas, which have the most critical housing shortages.

As Mexico races toward the next century, its economy is picking up some serious momentum, and business is terrific. Collateral needs, such as housing for the growing numbers of Mexicans entering the work force, are of concern to the government, employers, and the workers. A solid company with a track record, a product, and a plan will be welcomed into the area of low-cost housing. This opportunity will probably begin at the concentrated border areas and gradually expand to Mexico's other densely populated areas.

SHOPPING CENTERS

More and more Mexicans have more and more disposable income as the economy grows. With no end to this growth in demand for consumer products and services in sight, the shopping center industry is another terrific opportunity. In the past, most people were too poor to buy anything but the bare necessities of life, which they purchased at marketplaces or at one of the Big Five retail stores. There were so few very rich that shopping center construction was hard to justify.

The new middle class is demanding more: upscale department stores, restaurants, franchises, and the like. And they want these services nearby and convenient. The U.S.-style shopping centers are the rage. From Toluca to Mexico City to Cancun, megacenters are under construction to fill this demand; the tiny malls of the past are no longer in vogue. These new centers include hotels, restaurants, upscale shopping, movies, offices, and much more.

The face of Mexican consumerism is changing rapidly, and the shopping center developers are riding the wave of new prosperity. Billions are being invested in this area, with certain profits to follow. Investors seeing shrinking margins elsewhere in the world are spotting Mexico's shopping centers as a field with huge growth potential. As with many other of Mexico's incredible opportunities, the time to get established is now.

LONG-DISTANCE PHONE SERVICE

We know from the growth of Telmex that communications is an area of opportunity for the 1990s. Without modern intra- and intercountry phone service, Mexico cannot hope to meet its economic goals. By the mid 1990s Telmex will be what AT&T was in the United States prior to deregulation.

One basis for the government's modernization and privatization programs is competition being a good thing. Mexico learned that protected industries with no competition became bloated and unprofitable. All of Mexico suffered from such stagnation. Privatization has proved that competition makes for leaner, more efficient, and more productive industries.

All of Mexico's privatization sales have provided for a protected breaking-in period so that the newly privatized industries can get a foothold before competing with foreign companies. Telmex' breaking-in period is five years; and it began in 1991. The government can extend the protected period if it chooses to do so, but this seems unlikely given current policies.

This is no sure thing, but the opportunity for the lucrative field of providing long-distance service on a competing basis looks probable. The U.S. companies in the field would be well advised to begin subtle lobbying efforts and readying plans for entering this new market.

DO-IT-YOURSELF HOME CENTERS

One gauge we use in determining the next hot idea for Mexico is: What makes our guests from Mexico say "wow?" For years they were amazed and envious of our neighborhood Price Club. Now Price Club is changing the face of Mexican buying. So what's "wowing" them now? The huge do-it-yourself home centers. Many such companies in the United States are enjoying a period of high profit and fast expansion. Their next logical step is Mexico.

The growing middle class is increasingly able to afford their own homes. As Mexico's economy further stabilizes, more financing will be available, making even more Mexicans eligible for home ownership. And they want the same thing we do: a little nicer place to live.

Visit one of these do-it-yourself centers in the United

States on a Saturday. You will see long, long lines of customers with carts full of purchases. Here is a can't-fail opportunity for a fast-acting U.S. company.

RESTAURANT EQUIPMENT

Two unique situations have given impetus to a burgeoning demand for restaurant equipment: foreign tourists flocking to Mexico in record numbers and increasing free trade raising the disposable income of many Mexicans. A prime opening in the market for the U.S. restaurant equipment vendor/manufacturer exists because there is limited production of such material in Mexico itself despite the increase in demand. Equipment manufacturers can export to Mexico, set up a distribution facility in a central location, and then develop a marketing network to serve the country. On a somewhat grander scale, an assembly plant can be set up south of the border. We have looked at the rules and know the demand.

Used restaurant equipment (low mileage) could be another interesting profit opportunity. In the United States 9 out of 10 restaurants fail within the first year of operation. These failures leave unhappy lenders with some pretty new equipment. Through the lenders themselves or at bankruptcy auctions, these items usually cost only about 10 to 15 percent of their original cost. Put together the demand with this well-priced inventory via some pretty creative networking on both sides of the border and you have an incredibly profitable venture.

The Mexicans love fine dining, and tourists always seek new places to eat. The restaurant equipment field will grow along with disposable income and tourism throughout the 1990s and into the next century.

Sports Teams

Mexicans have always had a strong interest in sports. The country has hosted the World Cup of Soccer and the Olympic Games. In a recent interview, a Mexican government official announced new and even stronger government support of sports. The goals are twofold. First, a strong national sports program attracts favorable world attention, that is, more good public relations for Mexico, the new First World country. Second, the government wants the young people to have more modern-day role models to emulate. International television and promotion rights and the foreign dollars from sports teams are a third but not controlling issue.

Government is following the lead of business. Business in Mexico recognizes the potential profit and promotional benefits of televised international competition. A leading force in this drive is a group in Monterrey. Monterrey, close to the U.S. border and the richest of Mexican states, has broken ground on a $20 million sports arena.

Basketball is the coming sport. Mexico has had a basketball league for 15 years but now is taking it financially more seriously. Corporate sponsorship, licensing agreements, and television rights are becoming lucrative opportunities. An NBA franchise could be next. This is the goal of the Monterrey investors. With the newly reorganized Mexican Basketball Federation playing in exhibition games with invited teams from the United States, the investors intend to show that Mexico is a First World country in all respects. Professionally managed games with sellout crowds should convince the NBA that Mexico is perfect for their next franchise. Mexico is also seeking what Canada has already begun achieving with its baseball teams in Toronto and Montreal.

Government and business goals are quite compatible. The Mexican government wants to add to the national pride, bring in foreign dollars, and receive some good press for newly emerging Mexico. Business wants promotion, profit, and pride of ownership. As with many other areas of Mexico today, such a partnership of business and government will likely be quite successful. Watch for big opportunities throughout the 1990s for lucrative licensing, televising, and related profit ventures.

PURCHASING PRIVATE COMPANIES

Recently revised investment regulations permit U.S. ownership of a wide variety of businesses. If you are thinking of expanding your operations into Mexico or starting something new, consider that government statistics reveal that the owners of some 15,000 private companies with sales from $5 million to $20 million (U.S. dollars) are near retirement. The owners already have distribution, a reputation, a track record, and talented key people. In many situations it might be a safe bet to take over a company with its foot in the door. If your expertise is expansion and a company is well set in the area of opportunity you seek, buy a business. A retiring owner often has invaluable expertise and is delighted to share it. Look for a company that meshes with your present operation.

If you elect to follow this course, please consult your attorney because the rules for business transfers are different in Mexico. A few dollars spent now can buy you peace of mind later.

How do you find a company in your field? To get started, try all the methods you learned in the section on research in Chapter 5, and check with the larger banks and the Department of Commerce. There is big growth opportunity in Mexico. A company with a market position poised for success that is compatible with your business might well be your best move. You can save time and money with a going concern.

COMPUTERS, SOFTWARE, AND OFFICE EQUIPMENT

Look around your office. How many pieces of technology in it were available back in 1980? Black-and-white copiers were the norm, as were typewriters. Computers were an option or luxury at many offices then. Privately owned FAX machines were rarely seen. Cellular phones were available only to the rich or flamboyant.

At one time Mexico was at least 10 years behind us technologically. Import duties of up to 100 percent combined with a lack of capital kept much of Mexico's business community in the pre-1980 mode. But things are different now. New businesses are opening by the minute, older ones are expanding and modernizing, and the future looks great as business booms with Mexico's economy. The PCs, FAXes, copiers, and phone systems are much in demand. Many U.S. companies have already entered this market, but it is so unlimited that there is room for many more. Mexico's business community is undergoing a technorevolution. Banks are installing state-of-the-art computer hardware and ATMs. Phone lines are becoming more and more available, so private phone systems are in demand. Retail business equipment centers are springing up in the major metropolitan areas (often there is a waiting list for products). Manufacture in Mexico or export to distributors—either way, office and business equipment is a growing area.

Until recently, software companies considered Mexico an impossible market because copyright laws did not sufficiently protect the originators of the software. New regulations provide significant protections and penalties for violation. As more and more regulations are enacted, a software revolution in Mexico much as there has been in the United States since the early 1980s should occur. Chains of retail software sellers are already appearing in Mexico City, Guadalajara, and Monterrey. (I noticed one Mexico City marketplace vendor working with his laptop!) The market is pretty open now, but soon it will be a highly competitive one. Now is the time to make your move.

Mexico's economy is growing at an incredible pace. As the business community "techs up," a window of opportunity is opening for the astute provider of equipment and software. From cellular phones to FAXes, from PCs to copiers, this might be the best opportunity Mexico has to offer.

Oil Industry

Two areas of extraordinary opportunity exist in the oil industry: (1) serving the equipment and exploration needs of Mexico's Pemex, and (2) participating in the newly opening service station field. Many companies are already taking advantage of the opportunities in equipment and machinery. Pemex' expansion and exploration investments have slowed as prices have declined. Although capital is scarce, Pemex is still a huge functioning company. From 1986 through 1992, Pemex imported yearly from the United States in excess of $200 million worth of machinery and oil-related equipment.

The oil giant's needs for everything from pipes, fittings, and valves to fire-fighting systems should push imports from the United States over the $300 million mark. And worry not about Pemex's longevity or ability to pay because Pemex owns a controlling interest in several companies that are updating, modernizing, and exploring in little publicized and immensely profitable joint ventures outside Mexico.

Exploration and production joint ventures are already going on under the guise of "service contracts" in Mexico (remember, there is a constitutional prohibition against foreign ownership of oil businesses). Expect much more of this activity to occur since Mexico needs the money and the politicians have skillfully outmaneuvered privatization and constitutional prohibitions.

Mexico's service stations have been declared a nonstrategic part of the oil industry; that is, private profits are possible and encouraged along with outside investment. Presently, service stations can buy only from Pemex (who often buys from Arco), and only Pemex stations are allowed. Big changes are coming. The stations will soon be private franchises and will thrive in a competitive environment, which will mean better facilities (now they are pothole-ridden dumps) as the stations compete for business. Do not be surprised to see Circle K or Seven Eleven shops attached to these private franchises (another emerging area of opportunity).

As the service station sector opens to competition, quite possibly Shell, Arco, and others will be opening their own franchises within the next five years or at least selling directly to the Pemex franchisees. The sale of oil, filters, tires, and actual service are coming soon to Mexico's superstations of the future. By the end of the 1990s, the stations will be clean, competitive, and able to offer services they presently do not.

In the service station and other areas, the opening of Mexico's economy to competition will bring new opportunities for profit as businesses scramble to provide better service and products. From convenience store suppliers (or operators) to tire distributors, no one should miss this period of unprecedented opportunity. Make your alliances now for these opportunities.

PROFESSIONAL SERVICES

The continuing economic integration of the United States and Mexico has led to a need for various professional services capable of handling this new multinational activity. Some U.S. law firms are opening offices in Mexico, both officially and unofficially. Most of the large accounting firms either now have their own offices in Mexico or are establishing a continuous relationship with a compatible firm south of the border. Consultants, real estate brokers, and other professionals are all establishing Mexican locations in order to have a presence in this newly opened market.

Law firm activity is big for three reasons. First, competition in the United States is intense for clients increasingly unwilling to pay large fees for standard work; Mexico has less competition. Second, many of the larger firms represent multinational companies that until recently were uninterested in Mexico. To properly serve these clients, the attorneys are becoming established with local counsel. Third, Mexico's economy looks so good for the foreseeable future that it is too enticing a market for law firms to pass up.

The U.S. lawyers face seven additional years of schooling to become licensed to practice in Mexico. Because of this onerous requirement, only a handful of U.S. lawyers are also licensed in Mexico. Rules regarding practicing without specifically being licensed are somewhat looser in Mexico: you need not be licensed for many routine functions. Thus a U.S. firm can open an office, and the lawyers can call themselves attorneys, and handle routine matters. When a Mexican attorney is specifically required, they can associate one or more as necessary. The Mexican bar is somewhat disgruntled by these gringo semi-abogados (lawyers) entering what they perceive as their home court. Despite the outcries of unfair and incompetent competition, the Mexican government has already officially chartered several U.S. firms, allowing them to open Mexican offices. Many other firms are opening without the benefit of such a charter, and literally hundreds of firms are making working arrangements between Mexican law firms and their own in the United States. Now might be a good time to get your law office open in this not very restrictive environment. If increased regulation is enacted, your office, already established, might be grandfathered in.

The big accounting firms and the better small ones are not ignoring the action either. While Price Waterhouse is the only U.S. firm allowed to use their U.S. name in Mexico, the other firms are all represented, but use the names of their local licensees, for example, Ernst & Young and Coopers & Lybrand. In Mexico, the rules for the traditional accounting functions these firms perform are significantly different from those in the United States, so the professionals are far from interchangeable. Auditing and reporting are performed by Mexican-licensed CPAs, but these offices also offer consulting services, including executive compensation, mergers, acquisitions, and internal reviews. If your company is a second-tier U.S. accounting firm or a specialized small firm wishing to serve its multinational clients, be ready in Mexico; your clients will demand it. Visit Mexico, and at least set up a working relationship with a well-regarded firm.

Some of the larger strictly consulting firms have ignored Mexico and are now surprised to find that their clients need expertise. These firms are scrambling to establish themselves south of the border, but this is hard to do in a hurry. Other consulting firms had the foresight to open in Mexico years ago, such as McKinsey. Such companies now are already set up to serve the new flood of multinational clientele. And many small and specialized consulting firms also have a Mexican presence. If your firm is knowledgeable about the areas of environment, health care, financial services, petroleum, or communications, a great deal of billable business is available in Mexico.

The real estate business is suddenly exciting in Mexico. More people can afford houses, more businesses need different types of space, and even the government is upgrading many offices. Several new financing vehicles are on the market and many more are on the way, so real estate is an area to investigate. Both individual U.S. brokers and some nationally recognized commercial brokerage companies are establishing relationships in Mexico. Check with your lawyer about licensing requirements, but do not miss this opportunity if your interests are in real estate.

There is a tremendous demand for professional services in Mexico as the economy booms. Make your move now and be firmly established before your competition even notices.

ENVIRONMENTAL EQUIPMENT AND SERVICES

Mexico's environment is in sorry shape. Historically, little has been done; everything was just put aside until "tomorrow." Tomorrow is here now, and some severe problem areas need immediate solutions. The government has instituted programs in a number of areas to tackle this Herculean task. As a result of the new programs and regulations, a new industry providing equipment and technology to take on Mexico's environmental ills has been created. Let's consider how the Mexican environment got this way, what areas are the most polluted, what is being done, and what is needed.

Mexico's severe environmental problems are the result of decades of neglect. Population concentrations around the major cities (employment centers) have made matters significantly worse, along with a population explosion. Even the geography of areas such as Mexico City contributes to a steadily worsening environment. During the 1980s, the problem had to be acknowledged because significant health dangers could no longer be overlooked. As with Mexico's other ills, the problem was an effectively bankrupt economy, no money to improve conditions, and a hesitancy to limit what little industry was still functioning. And even had there been enough of a commitment or sufficient funds, the technology in the environmental field was unavailable. Further exacerbating the situation, protective tariffs and a closed economy prevented foreign environmental companies from entering the Mexican market.

Mexico City is among the worst areas for environmental disasters. Located 8000 feet above sea level in an area resembling a crater, the city's 3 million cars, 20 million people, and uncontrolled heavy industry are creating the possibility of a disaster beyond comprehension. Only slightly better off are the other population centers of Guadalajara, Monterrey, Tijuana, and other border areas.

Polluters in Mexico fall into four categories. First are the millions of cars, most quite old and ill-tuned. Second are the factories that until recently had absolutely no concern for the environmental effects of their production. Third is the people themselves. With very highly concentrated living spaces, millions are without the most basic sanitary needs of running water and effective sewage systems. Finally, new industries have created whole new types of toxic waste that has been dumped indiscriminately over the past decades. These causes all together create an environment that needs immediate help.

The good news is that government, business, and the people are not only admitting they have a problem, they are taking significant steps to solve it. But they need help in both equipment and technology. Regarding the auto pollution, several things are already being done. Mexico City has ordered that cars may be driven only five days each week. Forcing people to stay home, use public transport, or carpool is a step in the right direction. Also in Mexico City, and soon elsewhere, all taxis are required to have pollution-control devices installed as a prerequisite to permit renewal (that will affect 100,000 plus cars right there). Unleaded gas is just now becoming available in metropolitan areas; hopefully more rural areas will follow suit soon.

The auto pollution field needs measuring devices, pollution-control devices, and new technology. Oil-collection and recycling equipment and services in addition to the actual recycling of the steel from old cars are other open fields. The auto pollution–control industry is in its infancy; it will be a major growth area in the 1990s and beyond. (Alternative transport systems are on line for the year 2000 and beyond).

Heavy industry is another villain in Mexico's environment. Mexico's version of the EPA has closed some industries temporarily, closed others permanently, and given others deadlines to comply with new harsher regulations or move. Unfortunately, enforcement and further regulation are necessary to get these corporations to comply. The basic tenets of corporation law are against the environment. Corporations are created to make a profit and must answer to shareholders if they do not and for any expenditures not directly related to making such profits. Fortunately, with a boot from the government, the corporations are now racing to comply with new requirements. Any new capital goods that can help control industrial pollution are now seriously in demand. A number of consultants and attorneys serve specifically in the field of environmental regulatory compliance. If your firm can provide the technology to help Mexico's industry, you will be welcomed indeed (and of course you will make a profit).

The people part of pollution is a difficult problem that the government says is solvable, but more funds are needed to provide the basic sanitary services. As Mexico's economy grows, all hope that a significant portion of the new resources will go to improvement of these conditions.

Toxic waste disposal is an entirely new field. In many instances foreign polluters are required to reexport such waste. Long-term solutions are still needed, and government-funded studies are continuing at this writing. If your company can provide answers, the government would certainly encourage proposals. Private industry and government both have a strong interest in proper disposal techniques. Help Mexico, help the world, and help your company; the environmental improvement industry is wide open.

MISCELLANEOUS OPPORTUNITIES

Electric Power Production and Distribution Equipment

Mexico needs efficient power production and distribution. No real research and development went on in the hydro, petroleum, nuclear, coal, and geothermal power fields until the early 1990s because no money was available to fund such research. Presently, turbogenerators and turbines, and parts for both, measurement and control instruments, transportation equipment, and much more will be needed. Billions in capital improvement will be spent to power the reborn Mexico.

Agricultural Equipment

Mexico imports more than $250 million in agricultural equipment from the United States annually. We soon will see huge changes in the way Mexico's agricultural sector does business. Increased efficiencies and profitability are the goals. Mexico will need harvesting, plowing, cultivating, planting, fertilizing, spraying, poultry, and dairy equipment. This should be a growing area well into the next decade.

Machine Tools and Metalworking Machinery and Equipment

Presently Mexico annually imports more than $200 million worth of machine tools and metalworking supplies. Dies, molds, precision measuring tools, lathes, milling machines, and related parts and equipment are among the most desirable export items.

Medical Equipment, Instruments, and Supplies

Mexico now is able to spend more on the health care sector of its economy. As public and private facilities modernize and expand, more and more medical equipment will be required. Leading-edge technology to parts for x-ray machines will all be needed; for the manufacturer in the medical field, this is an open opportunity.

Road-Building Equipment and Products

Caterpillar Tractor is the major supplier of road-building equipment in Mexico. But there is room for other suppliers because literally tens of thousands of miles of roads need to be built and paved throughout the 1990s. New products for better and easier paving are surely in demand. Quality equipment is also a good export opportunity as villages, cities, and states begin the massive project of rebuilding Mexico's road system.

City and State Offices in Mexico

Many U.S. cities and states are eager to help their business communities grow and develop exports. Quite a few states now have offices in Mexico to promote foreign trade for their constituents, such as California. A helpful staff and a large library, together with good promotional campaigns, have helped many California businesses enter the Mexican market. From New England to Texas, cities and states are following California's lead in establishing these trade outposts. Whether you are in politics or business, this is an opportunity you should consider.

8

EXPORTING TO MEXICO

Exports are the number one growth area in the U.S. economy and, coincidentally, have been so since 1988, the first year of effectively open borders with Mexico. Now 8 million U.S. jobs are directly tied to exporting, many of these resulting from our more than $35 billion per year in exports to Mexico. Export volume to Mexico is increasing at over 10 percent (more than $3 billion) per year as more than one-third of U.S. manufacturers (130,000) are now exporting, a high percentage of them to Mexico.

Thinking of exporting your product or service? Mexico's 100 million consumers want U.S. products and services; they equate "quality" with "U.S. made." Mexican manufacturers cannot produce in sufficient volume or variety to fill this burgeoning demand, so the amount of U.S. exports of consumer goods to Mexico will increase.

Are you involved in the manufacture of capital goods? Mexico is rebuilding vast portions of their governmental and business infrastructure. Roads need to be built, factories modernized, computer technology added in all areas, and much, much more. More U.S. capital goods are needed, and with the rise in trade/investment you will find not only demand but also the ability to pay for such goods. What could be better for the U.S. manufacturer? Here is a huge new market, and very close by. Whether you are a veteran exporter or a small company just looking into exporting, Mexico provides tremendous opportunities.

This chapter first discusses the benefits to your company in beginning an export program. Next, we analyze just how exporting works, followed by information about product analysis. We cover how to gear up, conduct market research, check out the competition, and customize the product for Mexico. We then consider how to handle pricing issues, packaging, and shipping. We also cover the vital financing methods. Then we look at service, collections, and other issues particular to the export business. We conclude with possible alternatives to traditional exporting and list mistakes many beginning exporters make.

WHY EXPORT?

As Mexico slashes tariffs, reduces red tape, and streamlines the process of exporting to their market, thousands of U.S. businesses are entering the export market for the very first time, mainly for more profit. Let's analyze the different factors that make up profit to see all the benefits that exporting might bring to your company.

Simple accounting reveals the benefits of economies of scale. If you are increasing your number of units sold while fixed costs rise only slightly, not only are you increasing your profit, you can also price your product more competitively at home and in Mexico. Production and its variables are also factors in determining profit. If you properly plan your production for both the United States and for export, you can improve your overall productivity. You can significantly reduce or eliminate seasonal lulls involving underutilization of personnel and equipment by producing for export during the off periods. You create more jobs, increase productivity, and up the profits.

Mexico has not kept up with new products as a result of its protectionist policies during the 1980s. Mexicans have only recently heard about many of the products we are now bored with and that consequently are on the downside of their cycle. The Mexican people are excited to have access to these "new" U.S. products. Longer life cycles for our products increase profit on a per-product basis.

Losses/risks are often considered when actual profits are being determined. A broader customer base can also be of great value in this area. For example, suppose you have 100 customers. You lose one customer or the customer fails to pay; you lose 1 percent of sales. But if you expand your customer base through successful exporting and acquire 200 customers, the loss of one customer or its failure to pay is now only a fraction of a percentage of overall sales. You have a manageable problem rather than a crisis.

The tax advantages of exporting are best explained

by your tax accountant/tax attorney because they are very detailed and vary significantly by product. The U.S. government encourages these tax breaks because exporting helps our balance of payments.

From our point of view, the best reasons for exporting are more intangible. First, getting involved in exporting to Mexico is interesting as well as profitable. Second, you can learn many things in your international venture. Many of these marketing/finance/product lessons can be useful in your U.S. market; exporting gives you a more global outlook. Finally, exporting is good for the United States, creating more jobs for our people and a favorable balance of trade.

Export Product Analysis

Is your product a good candidate for export to Mexico? Your product analysis will decide if you should continue to the next step: getting your company ready to enter this exciting export market. Three categories of products are excellent possibilities. To check your exporting idea, ask yourself these three questions:

1. Is the product doing well here in the United States?

2. Is the product unique?

3. Did the product do well at some earlier time in the United States?

An affirmative answer to any of these questions makes your venture significantly more likely to succeed. Let's discuss each question in detail.

Product Does Well Here

If your product is a good seller here in the United States and there is a similar need for it in Mexico, then quite probably it will do well. To be sure, take the next step and analyze why you are doing so well at home before making the commitment to export. For example, what needs does the product serve? Who is buying the product? What is the customers' purchasing power? These are just a few of the factors you should consider. Then compare your findings with those from the same questions regarding the Mexican market. Does Mexico have a similar need to be served? Are there similar buyers? If so, do they make enough money to buy the product? If the two markets compare positively, your outlook is good. Finally, consider product alternatives. Is another product available in Mexico's market that serves the same needs and customers more economically? (This point is further considered in the "Evaluating the Competition" section later in this chapter.)

Unique Product

There are no product alternatives to a unique product. A product can be unique in Mexico but not in the United States. Say you are in a marketing environment of ever-increasing competition. Many other companies are copying your product or entering the market with very similar offerings. In any event, enough items are close enough to yours that your market share is seriously eroded. Your profit margins are razor thin, so you are looking for improvement.

If your type of product has not yet been introduced

to Mexico—it will be unique in that market—then your product has tremendous export possibility. While your competition fights it out in an increasingly crowded environment at home, you casually jump into Mexican exports and rule a whole new market. You outdistance your annoying competition at home because of your foresight in entering the terrific export market to Mexico.

Recently Terrific Product

In many respects, Mexican demand is 10 years behind ours here in the United States. For a long period, prohibitive tariffs and regulations kept U.S. products out of the reach of Mexican consumers. And those few products entering the Mexican market from the United States were often economically out of the consumer's reach because 90 percent of the purchasing power in Mexico was restricted to just 5 percent of the population; mass unemployment and poverty prevented the underprivileged from buying the products.

Now Mexico is a whole new world. The Mexican consumers are making more money, and they want to own what they have seen over the past 10 years. Here is an opportunity for a product that until recently was a terrific seller for your company. We are spoiled in the U.S. because of our leading edge technology. Consumers here demand that little extra button on the VCR, a computer that can complete a function in one second rather than two, and all the latest stuff in the catalogs. For a consumer who until recently could not even afford a color television, it is not so important whether or not the TV has "surround sound."

The same rationale for consumer goods applies to capital goods. (Here we are not speaking of the capital equipment needs of Mexico City or the like; the population centers are in many respects as technologically advanced as we are. Our analysis applies to those areas that only recently have begun rising from economic devastation.) Remember that for many years Mexican government and business have been repairing decades-old equipment rather than replacing it with new technology. A bank office that until recently handled all records manually would find a computer system that is not quite state-of-the-art most satisfactory. Last year's model of road-building equipment might be a godsend to a company accustomed to building streets by hand. Very basic medical equipment for a clinic could save many lives in an area never before served by even a full-time doctor. If you can provide such products that are fundamentally of good quality and useful but just not leading edge, at an economical price, your products will excel in the Mexican market.

GEARING UP

The U.S Commerce Department estimates that more than 80 percent of export failures are related to the exporting company rather than the product. Is your company fully committed to doing all it takes to be successful in the export market? Let's discuss what it takes so you can decide yourself.

First, define your goals. What do you hope to accomplish by exporting to Mexico? Are you seeking a broader customer base? A geographically wider distribution? Are you looking to lower unit production costs? Are you using Mexico as a major distribution point in your plans to export to South America? These and similar questions will help you specifically define your goal(s).

Next, determine if your goals and your plan to achieve them are compatible with the other goals of the home company. You and every member of your management team should discuss and agree on this main issue because it is necessary before you can take the next step of commitment.

To make exporting a successful reality, everyone directly or indirectly involved with the home company's decision to export needs to be ready to commit to a plan of action. Commitment does not happen overnight; it takes serious planning and often some hard work. The attitude must be "export positive." Production, personnel, and finance decisions and how the exporting function will fit into the overall picture of your company all need to be considered.

You have committed to development of an export market in Mexico. Now is the time to prepare an export plan. Four major factors will affect the plan: management, production, finance, and evaluation.

Management

You will have to consider who is going to manage the export venture and the team's relationship to existing home company management. In smaller operations the export team may be the same as the domestic management team, but in larger companies the two groups are usually different. They must plan ahead to work harmoniously.

Map out a personnel chart of who is responsible for what and to whom.

Production

Production is perhaps the most important part of your export plan. Ideally, your production for export will be done only during the downtime of your U.S.-market products, but production decisions may involve alternatives.

Finance

Where is the money coming from? How long will the effort take to pay for itself? Decide these matters in advance because decisions made later under deadline pressure using the "put out the nearest fire" approach will unnecessarily strain the exporting facet of your business.

Evaluation

Every business plan, especially one involving exporting, needs some mechanism for evaluating the management, production, and financial functions in light of actual experiences and changing conditions. Do not ignore this crucial step.

MARKET RESEARCH

You have determined that you are ready for change, the company is ready, and the goals are clear. Market

research is your next step. In Chapter 5 you learned how
to research your area of interest in Mexico. Magazines,
financial newspapers, and similar publications are terrific for an overview of a particular industry. Market
research is much more specific to your product. Your
preliminary research got you to this point; now it is
time to gather specific statistical information about the
market and how your product might be received in
Mexico.

One choice is to conduct primary research, which is
directly contacting people and businesses within what
you perceive as your potential market. This research can
be time consuming and expensive, but when properly
done, no better research information can be found. For
a small company with a limited market, such as new
ATMs for banks, primary research can be quite economical, involving only appointments and phone calls
within a limited (especially in Mexico) industry. A larger
company seeking to introduce a consumer product is
better off retaining one of the many consumer research
companies presently operating in Mexico.

An alternative to primary research but not as focused is secondary research, previously compiled statistical information relating to specific markets. This research can be significantly cheaper than your primary
research, but two cautions are in order. First, before you
rely on (or pay for) secondary research, be sure to find
out when this information was gathered. Mexico is
changing so quickly in every respect that information
accumulated more than one year prior is effectively useless. Second, find out who gathered the information and
what methods were used. As in the United States, Mexican research firms cover the entire spectrum, from exceptional (McKinsey) to the questionable.

Whichever type of research you use, be sure two questions are answered: What is the potential size of the market for my product? Who is my customer and what are its needs? Because so many factors must be taken into consideration, prepare a checklist so you do not overlook anything important. Consider your product, market, and customer in light of the following nine factors.

1. Mexico's economy—How healthy is the economy? What parts of it are most relevant to your inquiries? What are the forecasts? (Independent financial news sources are often more accurate in this regard than government statistics.)

2. Politics—In Mexico, politics are a significant force in business life. What policies of the current national, state, and local administrations might affect your product and the market for the product?

3. Regulatory environment and specific regulations—What are the current limitations? What regulations are on the horizon? Does your product fall into an area subject to significant government control? Does your product pollute? (If so, you have problems on the horizon.) Does it solve pollution? (New regulations requiring environmentally sound practices might create a market for your product).

4. Technology—What is the state of technological advancement in Mexico for your field? Is your product too advanced for the country's needs? (Maybe they have no equipment that can interface with your offerings.) Is the technology you are offering already there? Is there a specific need for your technology? The main question here is whether your product meshes with the existing state of the art in Mexico *and* answers a need within the market.

5. Cultural—Research into the cultural acceptance of your product is crucial. You learned in Chapter 2 what happens to companies that ignore the cultural factors in the Mexican market. Pay special attention here and use an expert intimately aware of Mexico's culture and how business fits into the scheme of things.

6. Market outlook—This factor is quite specific. If there is a need for your product, what does this specific market look like in the future? Are you talking state of the art with pressing need and demand, or do you want to export a product that is falling out of favor with the market?

7. Trends—This factor is critical and easy to overlook. Here is where older information can be helpful. Obtain whatever research was done five, four, or three years ago on the same subject and compare the figures and chart the trends. This forecasting can be a very valuable tool: a skyrocketing surge in demand in your market (or a continuous downward spiral) will be readily evident. Most older information is usually plentiful and cheap. Rely on it for evaluation of trends.

8. Market conditions—The subject of market conditions is best illustrated by an example. If you are planning to export restaurant equipment and the tourism industry is booming while local demand is increasing because of an increasing standard of living, you have a winner.

9. Market practices—Here again you will need a local with knowledge specific to your industry. What is standard in the industry? Thirty days no-obligation trial for this type of equipment? Free support? Updating at no cost? Any of these issues and a thousand more can

have definite effects on your profitability, so investigate market practices with the utmost care.

You must consider all nine factors to obtain a complete picture. Market research may seem like a lot of work, but the best researched products are the ones most likely to be the successes that many exporters only dream about. Good market research can save you money by pointing out inconsistencies in your expectations and spotting opportunities and special niches in markets that you might otherwise have missed. Spend the time and money to do the job right. Mexico is too big of a market for you to miss or to enter haphazardly.

Evaluating the Competition

Before you begin exporting to Mexico, you must study the competition. First find out who is already in the market you wish to enter, and then learn exactly what it is the company is offering. Your competition will be two different groups, one group the local (Mexican) companies presently offering a similar product, and the other group foreigners exporting to the Mexican market.

Group 1

To form a list of local competing suppliers, go to Mexico (or send your representative) and see who is selling what. If you can find the products for sale, information about the manufacturer and/or distributor is nearly always on the packaging. The Mexican equivalent of our

Yellow Pages is also quite helpful, as are banks, local chambers of commerce, trade associations, and some government offices. Trade shows are another excellent resource for determining your competition.

Group 2

Obtaining lists of fellow exporters with similar product lines is easier than you think. If you know your SIC (Standard Industrial Classification) code, the Department of Commerce keeps tremendous conglomerations of information. Trade shows and the other aforementioned resources can also be used to identify competing export companies. The American Association of Importers and Exporters also has interesting information available (see our Resource Guide).

Most companies will describe their product lines and advise you of upcoming additions if you simply call and ask them. A few days later, catalogs, information sheets, advertising, and sometimes even samples will arrive in your mailbox. But more fun (and necessary for doing the job right) are visits to competitors' plants and attendance at trade shows. Salespeople provide a continuous flow of information, often not stopping until you buy something or until they have revealed every last company secret. By shutting up and listening and asking an occasional probing question to keep things going, you should be able to get all you need.

Differentiating Your Product

Unless you have a unique product, you will have competition. Now that you have learned how to find out what the competition offers, you need to decide if you can compete. This decision making involves looking at your offering and differentiating it by category.

First, consider price. To make a profit, how much will you need to charge for your product? Exporting involves many pricing factors. As pricing relates to competition, just remember that you must be within the range of other companies with similar offerings. (Pricing is further explained in a later section.)

Next, determine if your product can be differentiated by quality. Coming from the United States your product has the perceived advantage of better quality than goods produced locally. This quirk is based more on historical production standards than present-day reality, but it does exist, so use it. Is your product actually of better quality than that of your competition? You need to know because your customers will be most interested.

Consider utility. Is your product as useful as your competition's? In what ways does your product better address the needs and wants of a customer? No matter how good the quality or attractive the price, if the product does not do what the customer requires and as well as competing products, no one will buy it.

After-sale support and service are important for many products. What does your competition offer? Can you compete? There are often involved issues when you are in a country other than your own, and they are critical in your competitive analysis.

Mexico is a terrific export market. In the United States, every industry is crowded, but there is a tremendous amount of room for growth in Mexico. And in many areas there is still very little competition, so this is a good time for you to enter the market and beat out your competition. Note, however, that Mexico's businesses are rebuilding and thousands more U.S. companies are entering the market. Competition analysis is not only crucial prior to entering the market, it should also be an ongoing effort.

PRODUCT CUSTOMIZATION

Often your product will have to be adapted for it to be an ideal candidate for the Mexican market. This adaptation is a standard consideration for exporters anywhere in the world. Your market research should have identified what the ultimate consumers want from the product. You will have to consider the tastes and needs of your market in determining potential changes for making your product perfect for the market.

In Mexico, as in any foreign market, buyers tastes are different. Your research should identify preferences in the areas of design, color, size, and the like. Warranty considerations are also a factor. How important is a service program? What do the customers expect? Can you provide the service? You must also analyze your product as it relates to the customs that are unique to Mexico. Incorporate all these factors into your business plan for product adaptation.

You must also look at concrete needs. Government regulations are a given. You will need to know health, environmental, safety, and even types of measurements required (metric?). Your attorney will help you review the relevant regulations; the Department of Commerce often has booklets for exporters on just this subject.

Any geographic or climatic effects that might require product adaptation have to be considered. And what about the level of education or the standard of living in your market area? Is your product too sophisticated? Can it be adapted to be more appropriate?

The final questions you must ask relate to physical and structural needs. These are effectively design considerations. If your product is electric, is it compatible with Mexico's power systems? What about measurements? Metric tools and standards are used everywhere except in the United States. Can your product be used or serviced in this regard?

You must consider all or some of these questions in deciding if your product has to be adapted for entry into the Mexican market. Since products range from major capital goods to small consumer items, it is impossible for us to list here every possible consideration. But the above groupings should get you on the right track; from there, your market research and the government regulations can guide your decisions.

Here is a tip that many exporters to Mexico learned the hard way: enter Mexico's market with just one or two products at a time. All products have unique considerations and problems. With each product entry you will get a bit smarter, and it is better and cheaper to learn a little at a time. With each product you will find entry easier.

Finally, do not miss the bottom line. Your thorough analyses will not help you at all if you do not check the cost of each possible and necessary adaptation to your product. If conversion or repackaging is not cost-effective, why do it? Try another approach. The knowledgeable exporter knows that product adaptation is often necessary if a product is to be successfully marketed. Do

research in this area and save yourself money and achieve
great returns.

DISTRIBUTION

Now you need customers to purchase your well-
researched can't-miss product. You have two choices:
handle the distribution function yourself (direct exporting) or bring in another company (indirect exporting).
Let's consider the pros and cons of both direct and indirect distribution.

Indirect Exporting Distribution

Indirect exporting distribution is through an export management company (EMC) located in the United States.
These companies already have distribution networks in
place; consider them similar to sales reps. Although you
lose some control in this situation, you have immediate
access to a broad range of customers. The export management company, at your direction and by the terms of your
agreement, takes your product and offers it to distributors,
wholesalers, and retailers, and directly to consumers if appropriate. Ideally this company will have experience with
similar, noncompeting products, so its network in place
is as good or better than any network you could build
yourself. The EMCs solicit orders and negotiate on your
behalf; you fill the orders, and either your company or the
EMC arranges for shipping.

Smaller exporters find these EMCs perfect and well
worth the cost (EMCs are paid a percentage of your take).

Often these small manufacturing companies have neither the resources nor the desire to mount a thorough and effective marketing and promotion campaign in Mexico. Hundreds of EMCs in the United States deal in products for Mexico. Interview many until you find just the right fit. A good EMC can make your business succeed beyond your expectations, whereas a bad one can get you into all sorts of trouble.

Direct Exporting Distribution

In direct exporting distribution, your company handles its own distribution. However, this does not mean that someone from your office has to knock on consumers doors; help is available.

To set up your own direct export distribution system, first evaluate your product. Find a foreign agent, a rep, or even a person who is a combination of services, to set up customers at the distributor, wholesale, and retailer levels.

Directly exporting your product gives you more control and more profits because no middleman is involved. The downside is setting up your distribution network from scratch, but many reps and distributors already have a customer base.

Directories of foreign reps and distributors are available through the Commerce Department. Or visit trade shows, go on trade missions, and do research to find these people. Do not be in a hurry to make a deal, and have your attorney check out the agreement before you sign. (Particularly be sure that the rep or distributor cannot also represent your competition.) Some companies

present their product at a trade show in Mexico; they
advertise for distributors to visit their display.

PRICING

How do you price the product? You cannot just add
shipping costs to your domestic price. Eight factors regarding pricing must be considered.

Competition

You must find out what competing export companies
are charging for their similar products. Next, research
what Mexican companies charge for competing offerings. These data give you a range to consider, but such
information is by no means set in stone. Depending on
your objectives in the Mexican market, this information
may be more or less important.

Cost of Production

The cost of production for export encompasses many
variables: overhead, R&D (research and development),
business research, traveling to Mexico, commissions,
consultants, legal advice, freight costs, and product-
modification costs. These are many elements to analyze
for your business plan, but you are better off considering
them now and doing the plan right. Once you are in the
market, price changes are most difficult and sometimes
impossible to introduce.

Demand

Mexicans are skeptical now of "new and improved" products because of the conduct of many state-controlled businesses during the lost years of protectionism. When those businesses needed more profit, they cut down on quality or raised the price. Thus, in determining the demand for a product in Mexico you must factor in skepticism. Consider what the market will bear without complete reeducation; simplify the design if necessary to keep the cost down. Once you earn a reputation within your market, you can introduce upgraded models at increased prices.

Discounts

You know from your experience in the United States that there are many price levels. You sell to a distributor at one price, wholesalers at another, retail stores a little higher, and the ultimate consumer at full retail. To determine the price of your product, do not forget to plan ahead for trade discounts. You must include a projected percentage breakdown of each level of sales, for example, wholesaler and retailer.

Allowances

This often overlooked area takes dollars right off your bottom line. Plan for allowances in your pricing because they are a fact of business life. In exporting, the goods travel farther, and communication is sometimes unsuccessful. No matter how much care you take to do things perfectly, products will arrive damaged, late, not of the size or style ordered, or undergo other problems specific to your product. Also, allow for a larger amount of allowance problems initially. As your experience increases and you get to know your customers' requirements, the amount of allowances will go down.

Flexibility

In Mexico, once you establish your price points, there is very little flexibility. Annual changes of moderate amounts might be well received, but more often the downfall of your product will result. If you enter the market at too low a price and later try to raise it, you may well lose your customers. On the other hand, if you begin at too high a price, you will miss out on new-product interest and will have to spend a lot on marketing to get buyers' attention a second time.

Government Regulations

In a few businesses in Mexico, price controls are still in effect, which is something to consider early in your exporting analysis. Another regulation that might affect your entry into a particular market is a permit. One factor they consider is the fairness of the price. But now so few products require any sort of approval that this will soon be a moot consideration.

Objectives

Do you want to take over an entire market? Are you just entering a limited market as a way of testing the waters?

What are your long-term goals for this product? How do
these goals relate to future anticipated products? You
must review your goals and objectives before making a
final price decision. Do not be lazy. Pricing is vital, so
give it the consideration it deserves.

QUOTES

This and the following section on financing will take
the mystery out of some of the financial details of exporting. You must understand basic terms to profit from
your new exporting venture.

When you make a sale to a buyer in Mexico (or
when one calls for pricing information), you will be
expected to give a quote. In exporting, a quote means
more than just a price. It begins with your providing a
very detailed product description. This detail is of great
importance so that no misunderstanding which might
affect your getting paid later on will arise.

Also include an expiration date, a date that the
quote is good until. Ideally, you will also include a state-
ment that prices are subject to change without notice;
when the caller places a firm order to buy, you can then
confirm the price and terms.

Also include the weight in your quote so that the
buyer can determine shipping charges and transportation requirements. The volume of the merchandise—for
example, how many cubic feet—is also relevant. Your
buyer will also want to know where to take possession
of the merchandise and what is included in the price.
FOB (free on board) is used to designate the location and
coverage. FOB [your name] (the exporter's) warehouse

means that no transportation will be provided. This is
the price at your factory, and anything additional
regarding transportation and services is extra. The term
FOB port of export means the cost of getting the goods
to the shipping facility is included in the price. FOB
buyers warehouse means that the goods are delivered to
your buyer's door at your expense.

Terms are an important part of the quote. Do you
expect advance payment? Irrevocable letter of credit (discussed below)? Are you extending terms or financing
assistance? Whatever the arrangements, include them in
your quote. Your buyer will also want to know when the
goods can be shipped. Are the goods in stock? Do they
take 30 days to produce? 60 days? Include this information in the quotation.

Thus a "simple" quote involves much information.
Include all the information just discussed together with
information specific to your product in your quote.

FINANCING AND GETTING PAID

When you ship your goods to Mexico, how do you guarantee payment? How do you obtain working capital to
fill a huge order? How do you obtain letters of credit?
How might your state's export assistance program help
you and your buyer find money to complete a transaction? Here we discuss the various ways to finance your
program and how to ensure payments.

The Export Import Bank (Eximbank) of the United
States is a resource you need to be familiar with. This is
a government agency charged with financing exports.
They do little direct financing, but their guarantee pro-

grams effectively achieve the same result. Under their working-capital guarantee program, you receive funds for your export-related needs (for example, receivables, inventory, payroll) from a commercial bank, and Eximbank guarantees 90 percent of that loan. Because they face little risk and with Eximbank's help for the processing, banks are quite willing to participate in this program.

Eximbank also provides a different type of guarantee for exporters of capital goods (big stuff) or exporters involved in huge projects requiring a continuous and significant supply of goods or services. These guaranteed loans are either short-term (1 to 5 years) or long-term (5 to 10 years). They are terrific for exporters of capital equipment and make the transaction significantly more doable from a buyer's point of view.

Why does everyone in the export business want an LC? An LC is a letter of credit, the preferred and most often used method of payment in export transactions. Let's look at how an LC works step by step, learn what can go wrong, and discover how to avoid these problems.

Your buyer's Mexican bank issues the LC and sends it to your bank. The LC says in effect that "we assure payment subject to the following conditions." Your bank (the advising bank) then advises you that they have the LC. The principle behind an LC is for a third party, the bank, to hold the money until the buyer is guaranteed he is getting the goods and that they are what he ordered. Your bank will charge you a fee for "advising"; do not confuse advising with guaranteeing—your bank is promising nothing. Your guarantee is from the Mexican bank.

If you want more assurance, you can obtain (for a fee) a "confirmation" from your bank, which means that your bank promises that payment will be made. But practically speaking, your bank will never pay until they receive funds from the Mexican bank.

Now, having been advised of the LC, you go ahead and ship the goods. You take your shipping documents to your bank, which forwards them to the Mexican bank. Absent problems, you then soon get paid (but never as fast as you think).

This system works well overall, but you do need to cover yourself. First, no bank guarantees anything. You need to avoid a "discrepancy." A discrepancy is the single worst word you will ever hear in an export letter of credit transaction. A discrepancy means that you are not getting paid. There are three types of discrepancies.

A typical discrepancy is late shipment. The LC specifies that the goods must be shipped on or before a specific date. If your shipping documents show that shipment is even one day late, you have a discrepancy (even if your buyer agreed to the delay on the phone). The LC is thus invalid. Your buyer can walk away from the transaction (remember that the goods are already on their way to Mexico, so you are in deep trouble). To prevent this situation, if it seems that you are going to be late in shipment for whatever reason, have the LC amended to indicate the new shipping date.

Another discrepancy is late presentation of the documents to the bank. A specific time period is provided for document presentation. If you are late for any reason, you might not get paid.

A particularly irritating discrepancy is when the documents do not describe the goods the same way as the LC does. Banks can be quite nit-picky on this issue, so be careful. Have a specific set of words on your original quote, use these same words on the LC, and use the very same words on all shipping documents.

On any of these discrepancies, your buyer will typically "waive the discrepancies." This solution fixes the problem but takes longer, adds more paperwork, and raises bank fees. Always watch for discrepancies. Remember, your buyer can walk away from the transaction, leaving you with goods on their way to Mexico at your expense. You then must find another buyer, pay for the return of the product, or give the buyer that walked away such a tremendous allowance that he will take the goods despite the discrepancy.

Another issue to consider is that a buyer will typically require "inspection" of the goods prior to the LC being paid. You should insist that the inspection take place prior to shipping. Third-party companies perform this specific service. They then issue a preshipment inspection certificate that your bank will readily accept, thus satisfying the inspection requirement in the LC.

Other help to finance your export transaction(s) is available. It is in a state's best interest that your business succeed in exporting because your success means more jobs and more taxes. Therefore, many states have established export finance programs. Six states at this writing directly finance export transactions, and another nine states have guarantee programs. In either event, you can get welcome and much needed financial assistance. Usually this help consists of a short-term loan for one transaction at a time, or, if you have a continuous exporting program, a revolving line of credit. Call your state capital to see what programs are available for your company.

9

Importing Opportunities for Individuals Starting Small

Furniture

Want to have some fun, furnish your house in Mexican colonial for free, and develop a terrific import business with a nominal cash requirement? Try importing handmade furniture from Mexico. Let's look at the types of furniture available, where to find the manufacturers (not just the middlemen), problems you might encounter and how to avoid them, prices you can expect, and how-to tips, beginning with your first buying trip and ending with the arrival of your first shipment in the United States.

Types

Seven types of handcrafted furniture are unique to Mexico: (1) cantara stone, (2) distressed wood, (3) raw marble,

(4) equipal, (5) wrought iron, (6) old wood, and (7) detailed handcarved wood. Some pieces of furniture are made of a combinations of these raw materials. The cantara pieces are often ornately carved stone. Distressed wood furniture is usually made of pine that has been treated (or abused) in some manner to look like old wood. Raw marble is plentiful in Mexico and used to create classic styles. Equipal is a leather piece of furniture, like a chair, with a willow or cedar base (usually crisscrossed). Wrought iron is used for coffee tables, bar stools, chairs, and the like. Another popular furniture-making technique involves using wood from very old barns, stables, and other buildings. This old-wood look is what the distressed-wood makers are trying to copy. The detailed handcarved pieces from Mexico are known worldwide; weeks and months are spent making an individual piece just right. While U.S. makers are gluing on "the handcarved look," the Mexicans are doing it the right way.

Areas

Handmade furniture is available for sale throughout Mexico. Generally, the closer you are to a major tourist area, the higher the price of the furniture, so if you want to buy commercially, you will not be buying in Cancun or Acapulco. Mexico City has some terrific furniture makers, as does Cuernavaca (45 minutes outside Mexico City). Just 30 minutes away in Puebla are several of the "major" rustic wood manufacturers. For the equipal, Guadalajara is the place. Tlaquepaque, just 45 minutes from Guadalajara, has many equipal sources as well as wrought iron. The cantara stone is best found in Chiapas, and for the true artisan handcarved pieces, go to San Miguel de Allende.

Problems and Solutions

Mexico has a particularly pesky wood-eating beetle that often finds its way into furniture and catches a ride to the United States. You should avoid this beetle at all costs because the only way to kill it is to have your container tented and gassed (about $800) (and heaven help you if the furniture has already been distributed to peoples' homes). The beetles look like inch-long manila-colored worms. You can always tell if they are hiding in the wood by the little piles of sawdust they leave behind while burrowing though furniture. These bugs are not a problem if properly treated. The larger and more reputable producers have gassing rooms; always ask to make sure. The better suppliers also do not skip the treating step in the interests of speed. Pay a little more to make sure it is done right. Visit factories and look at treatment rooms.

Cracking is another problem. Because most of the wood used is pine, the furniture maker needs to use seasoned wood. Recently cut or still-damp wood will cause you no end of troubles as it dries because it shrinks and/or cracks. If the wood is dried artificially, it expands when delivered to a moist climate. Sticking drawers or cracked tabletops can ruin your business, so watch out. The furniture makers who know what they are doing use properly seasoned wood, so you have very few problems. Do your research and ask questions, and ask to talk to customers who have been buying from the supplier for more than one year.

Consistency of supply and quality is another issue. Understand from the beginning that the handcrafted furniture of Mexico is a cottage industry, which means that no big factories are turning out one piece after another. The largest facility may have 20 workers, each able to do any job interchangeably. This system makes for some unique pieces, but there are problems with small suppliers. They can be late, quality can vary from one worker to the next, and financial problems can arise. Our best advice is to always have a backup supplier, buy from several sources at all times, and never get yourself into a supply contract situation here in the United States. Too much can go wrong when dealing with a variety of small suppliers. We had one supplier with a breakdown, another was kidnapped, the unions closed another, and another could not get materials because he did not pay the last time. If you go in person, communicate in an understanding manner with your suppliers, and never rely too much on any one supplier, you will do well.

Prices

If you buy from the actual furniture maker in Mexico, the prices are incredibly low, especially if you purchase in commercial quantities on a regular basis. For example, a beautiful distressed wood armoire bought in Puebla for $200 will retail at decorator's showrooms in the United States for $2400 and more. If you are importing to retail these items, you can sell them at $900 and always be out of stock. If you are importing to wholesale, smaller stores in the United States will gladly pay $600 to $700 for such a piece; larger multiunit stores will expect to pay $400 to $500 because they are buying in quantity, at least 10 at a time.

Prices and quality vary widely, so you should have a "local" with you. Learn all about quality by visiting as many producers as your time permits, asking lots of questions, and being observant. Pricing is a different story because no fair trade laws exist in Mexico. Mexicans give better prices to their countrymen (assuming their countryman follows the rules of business etiquette).

Tips

Two annual commercial furniture shows are held for the trade. Get on the mailing list so you will be notified. See Expo Muebles (Furniture Expo). Go and see what is available. Some suppliers will not be there, but enough will attend to make it worth your while.

Never bring into the United States less than a truckload. The above-mentioned armoire by itself could cost $1000 to ship to the United States, whereas if you negotiate and use the proper trucking line, you can have a 45-foot truck for less than $4000. Buy enough to fill every last inch of the truck to make your shipping cost per unit (item of furniture) as low as possible; the Mexican lines do not charge delivery by weight.

Work out a consolidating arrangement with your shipper. In other words, the shipper will hold your small shipments at its warehouse until a full truckload is ready to go. Make sure your consolidating company counts the pieces as they come in. If they are wrapped, make sure the consolidator unwraps them before signing for them.

Only buy from the real source so you have more control, receive a better price, and avoid a double value-added tax (every time title passes, another tax is added, so a middleman can cost you more than just his percentage).

Some suppliers are better for certain pieces of furniture than others. Go through their full line and compare the quality and price of each item. Stick to what each supplier does best and what is priced well. Thus you may end up buying two items from one supplier but five from another, but you will be getting the best deal for each line.

Do not try to have a supplier build something to your specifications because something always gets lost in the translation. Do not ship in ocean containers; they are never watertight, so over time the furniture can be seriously damaged. Armed with this information and the guidelines in the rest of the book, you now know enough to begin a successful furniture-importing business. Whether you sell to stores or to the public, your profit margin is terrific, all for a low investment of capital. Anticipate a total cost of $19,000 to $27,000 for a truckload of furniture.

ART

Do you have an eye for art, a heart for profit, and not very much money? Want some fun, a lot of travel, and a little glamour? If so, then importing art from Mexico may be just the business for you. This is one field in which a very small investment can turn into as big a profit maker as you wish. You are limited only by your talent and desire to work. Here we discuss the type of art available in Mexico, where to find the best pieces, how to deal with the artists, how to export your purchases, and how to sell what you have imported into the United States.

First, you need to know what is available. For cost-effective, easy shipping with minimum damage, we recommend paintings, prints, and the like. This selection may seem limiting, but it includes a wide range of choices. You can always add sculptures, ceramics, and whatnot later on in your venture. Prices and quality vary greatly, and one is often not a reflection of the other. We think you will have better luck with the middle-range pieces. One or two very high-end items might tie up too much of your capital (not a safe position), and the low-end pieces are not worth the shipping cost (and there is little demand for them in the United States). As a rule of thumb, your original purchases should cost from $21 (you will be surprised what you can get for this amount if you know were to look and you buy from the source) to $400 (a $400 item can retail at a U.S. gallery for $2500).

You should buy directly from the artist, with no middleman involved. Look for artists who are not yet "commercial," that is, those who do yet know that their works can be valuable. Mexico City has two weekend art fairs at which literally hundreds of artists display their wares. You could begin quite a varied business from these sources alone. Guadalajara has a similar fair each weekend. Consider taking a cab to Tlaquepaque (45 minutes from Guadalajara) because many good artists live there. Cuernavaca and many other cities also have much to offer, but for the all-time best collection in one city, visit San Miguel de Allende, which is an entire city of artists and artisans. Unfortunately, many people know this, so artists are constantly receiving ego-inflating compliments from tourists with nothing better to do and subsequently increasing their prices. As a dealer, you need to find artists ready to discuss wholesale prices and seeking U.S. distribution. Wherever you begin in Mexico, your time spent talking to artists will lead you to other artists and other places. With a little luck and your good sense, you can discover some terrific art finds.

Once you find some pieces you want or an artist you wish to represent, your next step is to purchase a nice mix of what is available. No matter how sure you are of one particular artist, do not spend your money all in one place. Admit that sometimes you are wrong. And offerings in various styles, sizes, and price ranges will enable you to find a wider market for your pieces in the United States.

When negotiating with artists, you will find that some are greedy capitalists, whereas others could care less about the commercial value of their work and are more interested in their work being appreciated by the widest range of people. You need someone right in the middle—that is, someone who will not price herself or himself out of your market—yet with enough financial motivation to keep producing at reasonable prices. The more artists you speak with, the better you will become at negotiations in this interesting area. If one source does not work out, do not hesitate to go to the next. But do not burn bridges because during your next buying trip conditions may be different.

Before you make each purchase, consider how you are going to get your newly acquired inventory home. A 10- × 20-foot sketch is a tremendous buy at $200, but shipping costs will make it prohibitive. Buy sensibly from a shipping standpoint. For framed items (frames in Mexico are often beautiful and cost very little in comparison to U.S. prices), buy at least several of a similar size for best packing. For unframed items, just be certain that some sort of shipping tube will fit correctly.

Your export method depends on the size of your purchase. If you have just a few moderately sized pieces, most likely you can arrange to take them with you on the plane home. UPS may be your answer for larger volume. Next step up from UPS is a trucking line with the capacity to crate your purchases and consolidate with other shippers.

The exporting rules are easy. Just be certain that you are not purchasing artifacts because many regulations prohibit the export of cultural artifacts (these laws are the result of the looting of "still being discovered" Mayan ruins). Anything other than these historical treasures are within the handicraft exception and duty free.

Once you are home from the expedition, you have a number of choices for selling your treasures. Depending on the quality of the items, take your purchases to retail stores and/or galleries. If you have excellent offerings in the lower end of prices, consider furniture stores or other accessory shops. If your purchases are mostly upper end, the galleries are your market. Retail establishments will pay you in advance for the pieces, whereas galleries often will offer only a consignment basis. Obviously full payment puts you back on the road for another buying trip because your profits are in the bank, so that is the preferred arrangement.

Also consider retailing these items yourself. If you have an accessory shop or gallery of your own, the items will be interesting additions to your inventory, and customers love one-of-a-kind pieces, especially if you have a story to go with the piece.

Rather than selling to stores or having an outlet of

your own, consider exhibiting at fairs and shows yourself. Local libraries carry directories listing these shows nationwide. Low overhead and only a few days work per month make this an interesting choice.

If you want to go all out in the art business (which we recommend only after you have done a few buying trips and have gained some selling experiences), open a wholesale/retail outlet/gallery of your own. If you have already established yourself as a good source to stores in your area, they will come to you if your prices are fair. You can supplement sporadic wholesale business with retail sales from your gallery/outlet (which you can advertise at fairs and showings).

If you buy correctly, you can (at a bare minimum) justifiably double your investment to wholesale buyers (cost plus shipping times 2) or at a minimum triple your cost to retail buyers. There are also many spin-off opportunities if you seriously get into this business. You can expand into other types of art work (enter these markets slowly), contract for exclusive representation of artists in the United States, set up distributors in other states, and much more. Starting with only a few hundred dollars, dealing in artwork can be a pleasant pastime or a tremendously profitable business. Find your niche in the art import world.

10

BUSINESS ETIQUETTE

———

Webster's Dictionary defines etiquette as "the conduct or procedure required by good breeding or prescribed by authority to be observed in social or official life." In business, manners and propriety are critical. In international commerce, the customs are less obvious. Simple politeness is a good beginning, but knowledge of local protocol is critical. In Mexico, social and business decorum are prerequisites to respect.

HOW LONG HAVE YOU BEEN HERE?

In Chapter 2 we covered the importance of culture in Mexican business. Mexicans are very proud of their history, and they prefer to do business with people of similar interests. They are interested in you as a person and

237

in your commitment to Mexico, not just profits. They
determine if you have this cultural commitment to their
country by asking two questions. At every business meeting where you have just arrived from the United States
or elsewhere you will encounter these two questions before any other questions are raised or issues are discussed: (1) How long have you been here?, and (2) What
have you done? Your responses to these seemingly innoc-
uous questions will directly affect your success in a
transaction because what really is being asked is:

1. Have you been here long enough to take in some
    of our culture?

2. Did you have the foresight to allow yourself
    enough time to take in this not to be missed
    culture?

3. What have you done since your arrival that
    shows your appreciation of our tremendous
    country and culture?

Obviously, to start off on the right foot in Mexican
business, *always* plan your trip so you arrive a day before
your first meeting. During your flight, read up on the
culture of the city you will be visiting. Decide what historical or cultural landmark you would like to visit.
When you arrive, grab a cab and take in the sights.

You do not have to trek through the jungle to the
latest ruins (although this is certainly worthwhile); we
suggest only that you take advantage of the wonderful
opportunities to culturally enrich yourself. Just be sure
you begin doing so before your first business meeting—
you will be glad you did. Visits Mexico City's world-
renowned Anthropological Museum, the Ballet Folklo-

rico at Belles Artes, and other cultural pursuits; such pursuits have turned otherwise routine business trips into memorable occasions for many people. Remember, social talk comes first. And part of this social conversation will include your responses to the culture questions. Anticipate them, prepare for them, and earn respect.

MI CASA ES SU CASA

Business and social life are inextricably intertwined in Mexico. If you are lucky, during a visit to south of the border someone will say to you "Mi casa es su casa." Literally, this means "My house is your house." But there is an implied meaning well beyond the strict translation that creates an entire set of social/business rights and duties. You will never hear this expression in a formal business setting because it is too personal for that arena. And rarely will you hear it in a "first meeting" social situation, unless you are being very personally introduced, such as your best friend introducing you to her favorite cousin. Mi casa may come up in a business setting after several meetings; you are now in a social situation, such as being invited to a "no business" dinner at which spouses will be included.

What exactly does the expression mean? There is no specific definition; it is more an indication that you have been accepted. Any initial mistrust has been set aside, and now you will be treated as a friend. Understand that the phrase is never said flippantly. In business, Mi casa es su casa promises friendship, honesty, and bend-over-backward fair dealing, similar to the Japanese concepts of duty and honor.

If you and your business associates reach the point of dealing on a mi casa basis, you are in an ideal situation because there is a presumption of honor and friendship on both sides. Do not treat this offering lightly. More than the Mexicans' home is open to you—friendship and their world are also being given.

HANDSHAKES, HUGS, AND KISSES

Another phase of business etiquette in Mexico involves the protocol for handshakes, hugs, and kisses. Timing, delivery, and propriety are all important. Your knowledge in this area will certainly be a reflection of manners, breeding, and cultural awareness. A comfortable entrance into and exit from business/social occasions will leave your associates with excellent first and last impressions.

At the initial business meeting, standard U.S. etiquette rules apply—handshakes all around. "Hi everyone" is inadequate and considered quite ill-mannered. Be firm, and do not sweat. The second business conference involves a gender difference. In Mexico, women are treated like ladies; the "just another one of the guys" U.S. business rule does not play here. At this second meeting, if the atmosphere is relaxed, the U.S. businesswoman should extend handshakes and kisses on the cheek. The U.S. businessman should extend a handshake; if a woman you are dealing with advances to kiss your cheek, accept the kiss and return it. Note here that we are speaking of upper-level corporate or business owners. When greeting workers or functionaries, *never* go beyond the handshake stage. The greeting must be appropriate to the relationship.

The next rule is important in the United States but even more so in formal Mexico: Do not use first names until specifically invited to do so. Also, remember that pronunciation is different in Spanish so ask twice if you are not certain. Mexicans are accustomed to U.S. businesspeople having some language and pronunciation difficulties and will appreciate your taking the time to get their names right. We have all been in those situations where someone gets a name slightly wrong and during the entire meeting everyone is uncomfortable whenever the name is used. They are thinking, "Do we tell him or not?" instead of paying attention to your presentation.

In Mexico, business quickly becomes social, and it is at these social meetings that you will be put to the test. Mexicans understand that U.S. customs are different from theirs, so they expect you to be awkward regarding many social practices. Surprise them with your social adeptness. Upon arriving at a small social gathering, the man should kiss each woman on the cheek and shake hands with each man present. A U.S. woman arriving at such a gathering should greet each person, male or female, with a grasp of the hand and a kiss on the cheek. Both men and women should perform the same respective ritual when leaving the gathering. Understandably you will feel awkward, but everyone else will feel comfortable as you display your social finesse.

If you will be doing business in Mexico more than once, your business cards should be printed in Spanish or in both English and Spanish. This consideration reflects your long-term commitment to Mexico.

It is critical in Mexican business to be respected. Keep earning that respect by learning and practicing Mexican customs. Even if you are initially clumsy, your hosts will appreciate your efforts. Observance of seemingly unimportant social formalities makes a much more constructive impression than you think. These apparent informalities are among the more important customs for the generally reserved American businessperson.

TEQUILA POWER LUNCHES

A power meal is an entirely different concept in Mexico. Forget about our ideas of low-cholesterol, minimalist, nouveau, midday lunch meetings. South of the border, lunch—lengthy, heavy, and colorful—is the main meal of the day. Even the most fervent granola eaters cave in when faced with the opportunity of such culinary abundance. Here, lunchtime is for relaxation and to strengthen relationships. Initially, it is also a time when the Mexican businesspeople are taking your measure. Let's discuss the importance of lunch to business ties, acceptable and forbidden areas of conversation, special drinking protocol, and deciding who picks up the check.

For most of Mexico, lunchtime is from 2 P.M. to 4 P.M.—a full two hours. The only exception is on the border and in outlying areas where so much U.S. business is conducted that the local businesses conform a bit more to our time: 12 P.M. to 2 P.M. Regardless of when the lunch starts, however, it always lasts two hours. You may safely presume that all business grinds to a halt during these hours, so do not even bother to call a company then.

The business lunch in Mexico is very important. Few commercial matters are discussed. This meal is concerned with cementing friendships and business ties, so you will have to conform to the rules of decorum for the Mexican power lunch.

First, certain topics are considered acceptable for discussion at the midday meal: world news, general business climate, family and mutual friends, and specific business only if your Mexican host brings it up. Remember, lunch is a time for relaxation, so do not go beyond safe subjects.

Inappropriate subjects are: death, ailments (no whining), money problems, and catty gossip. Avoid these areas at all costs. Also be extra careful about your language: profanity and off-color remarks are much less accepted in Mexico than they are here. And they are extremely unacceptable in the presence of women or your host's family. It is better to be too cautious and formal than to risk offense.

Drinking, while falling from favor in the United States, is still a big activity in Mexico. Social drinking is the custom, so pay attention. Be especially wary if you are not accustomed to drinking at lunchtime. Also, very high altitudes, such as Mexico City's 8000 feet, amplify the effects of alcohol. Know your limits and do not exceed them. The sozzled U.S. businessperson is hardly the image you wish to portray.

Who pays la cuenta (the bill)? The rules in Mexico are similar to U.S. custom. Always expect a friendly argument over the check. At the first sign of tension, concede the point and offer your thanks. Any suggestion that your host might be unable to pay may be strongly offensive.

Gifts: Bribe Versus Thoughtful Remembrance

Again we are in delicate territory. Mexico is a formal
society; gift giving is not exempt from the requirement
of correctness. You need to know about tips, bribes, business gifts, and social offerings. The presentation and delivery of these items are also of key importance. Here we
review these topics and suggest appropriate gifts. You do
not want to commit a breach of social or business etiquette, like the gentleman who sent red flowers to a governor's wife as a thank-you for a social invitation. The
man's career is in ruins; he is a social pariah because in
Mexico red flowers are a symbol of witchcraft.

Regarding tipping, the "look how fast I got rich"
U.S. businessperson of the 1980s is out. In its place is a
slightly more conservative traveler. Do not revert back
and become the ugly American of gratuities: a 15 to 20
percent tip for cabs, waiters, hotel workers, and so on is
substantial and correct for good service. When appropriate, consider supplementing these tips with the U.S.
products suggested below. Remember, an unreasonably
high gratuity will not buy respect; Mexicans will take
your money and think you a fool.

Mexican business and government have received
bad press concerning bribes. The outsider pictures a land
of graft, kickbacks, payoffs, and the casually palmed
U.S. $100 bill. About 30 percent of this was true at one
time, but basically it has no place in today's Mexico.
Education has replaced brute force in politics, and talent
has overridden nepotism in government. As in any country, there is a measure of dishonesty, but nothing you

should be associated with. Maintain your integrity; avoid the enticement of apparent shortcuts. Over the long run, your reputation for honesty will take you much further and your profits will be greater. Do not even think about bribing customs agents or police. The only time money should change hands is for official services rendered or to pay a fine. Pay if it seems correct and fair.

The two types of business gifts are the incentive and the remembrance. The incentive is best explained by the example of the architect with whom we consult on occasion. His specialties are private estates for the gentry and small specialized resorts. In each case he deals with several contractors, all facing the mañana syndrome. Our architect has built a fine reputation for on-time work by offering incentives beyond money to his contractors. He establishes a realistic completion date, adds two weeks to the schedule, and presents a Rolex watch for finishing on time. The same amount in cash would not work; incentives stir new reservoirs of ambition.

The business remembrance is rarely personal. It is distinguished from the incentive by its de minimis monetary value. A manager (note, *not* an owner) of a company with which we do business has done a terrific job every time and put in that extra effort. He once mentioned an interest in chartering a sailboat for a tour of our East Coast. We did some research and unasked sent him a package of East Coast sailing publications, brochures on charters, and the like. Such a little effort on our part gave him a great deal of enjoyment. We often send plants (huge is important) to office workers who have shown us special consideration. Such a remembrance from a U.S. businessperson can be a source of great pride to a clerk or office worker. Remember that these are the people who often actually do the work for which you have contracted. The remembrance in a business situation is not personal but thoughtful and personalized. It is used for people in staff positions, not the owner.

The rules of gift giving have their own code in the upper levels of corporate business and with owners of small businesses. The basic rule is that gifts should be as to a friend, but "friend" in the formal social sense as it is used in Mexico. Monetary value is not an issue, although too expensive a gift might be inappropriate and may offend. Thoughtfulness and personalization are the important factors. You will find that you want to indulge in this custom because your new associates and business acquaintances welcome you in such a friendly manner.

There are many appropriate, special gifts for these situations. Certain American products are unavailable in Mexico or are absurdly expensive, such as a Butterfinger candy bar, which costs $2 in Mexico but only 50 cents here. Your friends could certainly afford the $2 but one bar does not mean that much to them. However, a box of 50 bars hand-carried from the United States is a special treat.

For some reason, the variety of cheese in Mexico is limited as compared to that in the United States. A wheel of Brie or two pounds of fine cheddar are always popular. Remember the importance of family: gifts of the latest in children's toys are well received, and when available in Mexico, they are often comparatively expensive. Always listen for people's favorite things. Gifts can range from U.S. electronic gadgets to Ninja Turtle underpants for the children. The right item for the right person at the right time is what you want.

Delivery and presentation are as important as the gifts themselves. Do not use the Mexican mail because the gifts will not get to their destinations. DHL, UPS, and Federal Express are your best bet. Even more impressive is to bring the gifts in person, which means so much more than an impersonal delivery service. Do this whenever possible. Present your gifts when least expected, and present them on a friendly basis, not as payment for friendship or services rendered. Much of this etiquette will become automatic as you fall in love with Mexico and its people.

In Mexican business and society you will get along by fitting in. Protocol and correctness apply equally to both areas, especially in the area of gift giving. Follow our rules to avoid embarrassment, and take the opportunity to make people happy.

PATIENCE + SENSE OF HUMOR = PROFIT

Here is the formula for your success and survival in Mexican business. Protocol requires composure under stress. Patience and a sense of humor will help you achieve this calmness. The U.S. businessperson is accustomed to vocally exercising authority and prompt action, but such behavior in Mexico might be perceived as ill-mannered ineptitude. The Mexican businessperson exercises the ultimate in self-control, using finesse to handle even the most trying of matters. Workers and friends respect this ability to the point that more results are achieved and greater profits are produced.

If you are a type A personality and a very prosperous businessperson here in the United States, do not think you can barge into Mexico and "Show 'em how it's done." Nothing will happen. It will be as if there were a brick wall between you and profit. Your workers will not like you, you will seem like a tyrant, and everything will go wrong.

Learn to maintain your composure by knowing what to expect. Due to a lack of education, even the hardest-working person will test you with petty tomfoolery and an apparent inability to immediately understand new things. Anticipate this. Establish a point up to where you will accept a certain amount of playfulness but beyond this point you may vent your wrath. Your workers will respect this boundary, and you will rarely have to become intolerant. When training personnel for new tasks, presume that everything needs to be learned. Go over each step of new duties several times. If the workers understand what you want and know how to do it, you will get better work than anywhere in the world. Be patient; exercise self-control.

Maintaining your sense of humor is vital. Mexico is a nation of strong individuals, so the U.S. concept of team effort goes out the window. In Mexico, your business will be like a machine having 1000 tiny cogs, each cog acting independently and requiring specialized attention. At the very beginning you should ask yourself "What new thing is someone going to totally mess up?" Prepare yourself for this eventuality. From the outside these screwups are often funny. If you can remove yourself from the immediacy of these countless "adjustments," you will survive the break-in period of any new business.

With the respect of your workers and associates you will accomplish great things in Mexico. Earn this respect by being tolerant and fair. Mexico is a different country, and the people are unaccustomed to our business practices. Some practices they will accept; others you will have to improvise. Inflexibility will end in failure, whereas patience and a sense of humor will lead you to profit.

11

SPECIAL OPPORTUNITIES FOR CANADIANS

For Canadians, Mexico is a veritable gold mine of trading and investment opportunity, easily accessible to the Canadian market by rail, ship, and road. The modernization of Mexico is creating a significant need for what Canada is especially qualified to offer.

In 1988, Canada began a program of increasing trade relations with other countries in North and South America. First was their historic Free Trade Pact with the United States in 1989. Next, in 1990, Canada's global outlook became even more far-reaching when they decided to join the Organization for American States, dealing primarily with Latin America. Finally, their participation in the North American Free Trade negotiations evidenced Canada's desire to become a part of a North American Free Trade area.

Canada's borders are already fairly open to the United States as the 1989 Free Trade Pact phase-in period for

tariff reduction proceeds. Mexico is a somewhat more
limited trading partner, but trade is expected to grow
with increasing speed throughout the 1990s. Current
Canada/Mexico trade stands at close to $3 billion per
year, with direct Canadian investment in Mexico at
another $500 million.

Communications technology, supplies for Mexico's
Pemex, agricultural products, and transportation machinery are Canada's chief exports to Mexico. Northern
Telecom, Star Aerospace, and Moore Corporation are
among the many Canadian players in supplying Mexico's
huge demand. Forward-thinking Canadian businesses are
pursuing new opportunities in the telecommunications,
forestry, and pollution-control fields. Together with
transportation products and oil-related hardware, these
areas have phenomenal growth because Mexican demand
is creating unprecedented opportunity for the astute and
informed trader.

The outlook for Canada/Mexico trade appears bright.
Each country's economy, production, and requirements
complement the other's. The geographical proximity of
the two countries as well as reciprocal economic needs and
natural resources will create a strong trading bond. Now
is the perfect time for Canadian interests to establish commercial ties with Mexico.

SPECIFICS

United States/Canada bilateral trade runs at about $200
billion per year. Canada/Mexico trade, on the surface,
pales in comparison at $3 billion annually. But Cana-
da's trade with Mexico only recently has been possible.

You are in effect looking at just the beginning of trade between the two countries. Until recently, Mexico was unfamiliar territory to the Canadians.

Telecommunications

Telecommunications is an area in which Canadian companies with their "high skill, higher technology" abilities can compete with any country in the world. Mexico's technology needs are enormous, and in the telecommunications field, several Canadian companies are already profiting from the opportunity. Giant Northern Telecom Ltd. is well into a $300 million contract to provide cellular communications equipment. Because the cellular concept is particularly hot in Mexico and the answer to many problems, this contract is undoubtedly one of many more to come.

BCE Ventures Corporation of Toronto was granted licenses to build several cellular networks. Quite profitable in themselves, BCE has been pleasantly surprised by such spin-off opportunities as sales of thousands of top-end cellular phones. A wide variety of customers use these phones, from wealthy rural ranchers eager for communications and the latest in cellular gadgetry to small "no phone" villages where one business buys cellular time and a phone and then lets villagers use the phone for a fee. BCE's quality work and great reputation in Mexico portend well for its future in this growing area.

Tourism

More than 550,000 Canadians vacation in Mexico each year, and many businesspeople travel south for commercial reasons. People from around the world are discovering Mexico's particular charm, and more and more Mexicans have the money and time to vacation. Canada's Four Seasons is opening one of their magnificent showplaces on the Reforma in Mexico City. Other establishments are sure to follow. Restaurants and franchise travel services should also investigate the possibilities in Mexico's booming tourist industry.

Transportation

Mexico's rebuilding of its transportation infrastructure has provided many business opportunities. The largest Canadian deal to date has been Bombardier Corporation's purchase of Concarril (railcar manufacturer) in a recent privatization sale. With 3000 Mexican workers and a $20 million modernization program under way, Canada now has a substantial presence in Mexico's transportation industry.

In transportation-related areas, Canadian companies have provided road graders for massive highway construction projects, and several other companies are bidding for contracts to provide goods and services in similar fields. Efficient transportation is a prerequisite for Mexico attaining true First World status. Big opportunities for Canadian companies will continue throughout the 1990s.

Manufacturing

Several Canadian companies are taking advantage of inexpensive labor in Mexico. Two notable maquiladora facilities are Canadian-owned, both producing auto parts: Fleck Manufacturing Corporation and Custom Trim Ltd.

Mining

In a recent privatization sale, a Canadian consortium came within inches of purchasing one of the largest copper mines in the world. But even without this purchase, Canadian Noranda has substantial interests in Mexican mining.

Banking

Canadian banks are joining U.S. institutions in trying to gain full access to the Mexican market. The Royal Bank of Canada, the Bank of Montreal, the Canadian Imperial Bank of Commerce, and the Bank of Nova Scotia are the leaders in this effort. By the mid-1990s, Canadian banks should have established more than just a token presence in Mexico.

Miscellaneous

Canadian firms have entered various Mexican fields: gold exploration, aerial mapping, prefab building construction, pollution-control equipment, digital imaging, cattle, and even the providing of yogurt machines.

Two success stories in other fields are Moore Corporation and Quebecor Printing Inc. Moore has been doing business in Mexico since 1949, but recently it was able to import some high tech printing equipment. Under previously restrictive tariffs it was impracticable to import such capital goods. Moore's expansion plans with this new capacity include increased government contracts as well as serving the business form printing needs of Mexico's growing business community. Quebecor is the second largest commercial printing company in North America. The company purchased a going concern in Mexican printing for about $10 million. An instant presence in the market, Quebecor sees their purchase as an excellent investment in the potential of the Mexican market.

INFORMATION

To find out more about entering the Mexican market, first use all the resources listed in this book. Also, consider that the Canadian government has resources specifically available to your company. External Affairs has sponsored trade missions to Mexico in the mining, plastics, agriculture, food products, and software fields. More such missions in a variety of different fields are on the horizon; contact External Affairs for information. Trade missions are a cost-effective way of meeting the right people in an efficient manner. Other resources to consider are the Canadian Exporters Association and specific trade shows held in Mexico.

APPENDIX A
MEXICAN HOLIDAYS

January 1   New Year
February 5   Mexican Constitution
March 21   Juárez' Birthday
Holy Thursday
Good Friday
(Entire Easter Week—Semana Santa—is spent celebrating)
May 1   Labor Day
May 5   Battle of Puebla
September 16   Independence Day
October 12   Día de la Raza
November 1   State of the Union Address
November 2   Day of the Dead
November 20   Mexican Revolution
December 4   Federal Employees Day
December 24   Christmas Eve
December 25   Christmas

Appendix B
Important Mexican Companies

Aeromexico One of Mexico's two major airlines. Privatized. Major competitor of Mexicana. Emphasizes business travel, does much Mexico/Europe business. Owns charter/cargo lines: Mextur and Mexpress.

Cemex Fourth-largest cement company in the world. Actually a holding company that controls a significant majority of the Mexican market. Construction industry in Mexico is doing great, so too is Cemex. Adding a $1 billion expansion. Exports quite a lot to the Far East.

Grupo Carso Holding company. Significant holdings in Telmex, copper, tobbacco, Sanborns, a wire and cable manufacturer, and an electrical motor and engine manufacturer.

Tamsa Makes tubing for the petroleum industry. Became major exporter after Mexican oil crash in 1980s. Is now returning its emphasis to Mexico as Russia and other countries dry up as markets.

Televisa Mexico's television giant, recently taken public. Getting more into cable and making purchases in foreign markets (United States, Argentina, Chile). Subsidiary company is VideoVisa, which controls a significant part of the videocassette production market, videocassette rentals, and distribution.

TELMEX   Privatized Mexican phone company. Accounts for a significant part of Bolsa's capitalization. Most successful ADR to date. Spending $2.5 billion per year in a rebuilding and expansion program.

VITRO   Mexico's largest glass company. Recently purchased the U.S. company Anchor Glass. Forty percent of its assets are outside Mexico. Owns part of Whirlpool.

CIFRA   One of Mexico's foremost retailers and holding company. Entered into a recent joint venture with Wal-Mart; in Mexico, Club Aurrera is similar to Sam's Warehouse. Holdings include retailers and restaurants.

COMERCIAL MEXICANA   Major retailer. Has a joint venture with Price Club. Very aggressive competitor of Cifra.

GIGANTE   Major retailer. In a joint venture with Fleming Companies, a U.S. wholesaler of foods.

Others include Herdez, Ford Motor Co., General Motors Mexico, Chrysler de Mexico, Rayovac, Sunbeam, General Electric, IBM, General Tire de Mexico, Goodyear, Gillete de Mexico, Kraft, Dupont, Shell de Mexico, BASF, Sherwin Williams, Johnson y Johnson, Bayer, and Colgate Palmolive.

APPENDIX C
FRANCHISES IN MEXICO

Acapulco Joe
Alphagraphics
Arby's
 International
Archers Industries
Athlete's Foot
Avis
Baby Gym
Barrocos
Baskin-Robbins
Bebe Express
Beefans
Beverly Hills
 Workout
Burberry
Burger Boy
Bye Bye
Century 21
Chazz
Club de Precios
Copiroyal
Dairy Queen
Danesa 33
D'Bebe
Days Inn
Denny's
Dollar Rent a Car
Domino's Pizza
Domit

Dorimimundo
El Pollo Loco
Embassy Suites
Emcyo
Esprit
Fester
Food Circus
Franquimdi
Fuddruckers
Giragrill
Gonher
Grupo Anderson
Gymboree
Hard Rock Cafe
Helados Bing
Helados Holanda
Hertz
Holiday Inn
Hoteles Mision
Howard Johnson
Ibaraki
Juvens
Kentucky Fried
 Chicken
Kwik Kopy
La Ferre
La Luna
La Mansion
La Tablita
Las Flautas

Laura Ashley
Levi Strauss
Manpower
McDonald's
National Rent a
 Car
Mexcel
Opticas Devlyn
Pizza Hut
Profution System
Proyecto Bryck
Radio Shack
Restaurante Niza
Roche Buvois
Rotualart
Shakey's Pizza
Shanson Frozen
 Yogurt
Showbiz Pizza
Sign Express
Subway
Sun Center
Super 8 Motels
Taco Inn
Thrifty Rent a Car
Toning Point
Trionica
VIPs
What a Burger

Appendix D
Government and Organization

Mexican Government

Form: Republic

Divisions: 31 states, 1 federal district

Head: President, one 6-year term

Congress: Senate (64 members), 2 members each state, one consecutive 6-year term only

Courts: Supreme Court of Justice, 21 lifetime members, appointed by the president

> 21 Circuit Courts, Supreme Court appoints judges
>
> 68 District Courts, Supreme Court appoints judges
>
> 31 Superior Courts of Justice (highest court in each state)

State Government

Governor: one 6-year term only

Chamber of Deputies: 9 to 25 members, no consecutive 2-year terms

Local Government

Municipios: 2400
Elect municipal presidents and councils to 3-year terms

States and Capitals

Aguascalientes—Aguascalientes

Baja California Norte—Mexicali

Baja California Sur—La Paz

Campeche—Campeche

Chiapas—Tuxtla Gutiérrez

Chihuahua—Chihuahua

Coahuila—Saltillo

Colima—Colima

Durango—Durango

Guanajuato—Guanajuato

Guerrero—Chilpancingo

Hidalgo—Pachuca

Jalisco—Guadalajara

México—Toluca

Michoacán—Morelia

Morelos—Cuernavaca

Nayarit—Tepic

Nuevo León—Monterrey

Oaxaca—Oaxaca

Puebla—Puebla

Querétaro—Querétaro

Quintana Roo—Chetumal

San Luis Potosí—San Luis Potosí

Sinaloa—Culiacán

Sonora—Hermosillo

Tabasco—Villahermosa

Tamaulipas—Ciudad Victoria

Tlaxcala—Tlaxcala

Veracruz—Jalapa Enríquez

Yucatán—Mérida

Zacatecas—Zacatecas

APPENDIX E
MAQUILADORAS BY CITY

City	Number	Employees
Agua Prieta	28	6,000
Chihuahua	61	29,000
Ciudad Acuña	44	14,000
Ciudad Juárez	320	135,000
Ciudad Obregón	3	1,000
Ensenada	33	1,800
Guadalajara	17	4,500
Guaymas	3	900
Hermosillo	22	5,000
La Paz	16	1,100
Matamoros	94	38,000
Mérida	28	4,000
Mexicali	154	21,000
Monterrey	83	16,000
Naco	6	1,000
Nogales	73	21,000
Nuevo Laredo	93	16,000
Ojinaga	1	300
Palomas	5	100
Piedras Negras	43	8,000
Reynosa	71	30,000
Saltillo	5	3,000
San Luis Río Colorado	12	3,000
Tecate	86	4,500
Tijuana	530	59,000
Torreón	29	4,500
Other Cities	30	10,000

RESOURCE GUIDE

ORGANIZATIONS/ GOVERNMENT OFFICES/ PUBLICATIONS

American Chamber of
Commerce of Mexico
Lucerna 78
Col Juarez
Del Cuauhtemoc
Mexico, D.F. 705-0995
(011) 52-5-705-0995

American Chamber of
Commerce of Mexico—
Guadalajara
Avda. 16 de Septiembre 730-1209
Guadalajara, Jalisco, Mexico
(011) 52-36-150-074

American Chamber of
Commerce of Mexico—
Monterrey
Piachos 760, Despachos 4 y 6
Colonia Obispado
Monterrey, Nuevo Leon, Mexico
(011) 52-83-48-7141

American Association of
Exporters & Importers
11 W. 42nd Street
New York, NY 10036
(212) 944-2230

California Trade and
Investment Office
Reforma 450 - 4th Floor
06600 Mexico, D.F.
(011-52-5) 208-5161

California Chamber of
Commerce
1201 K Street, 12th Floor
Sacramento, CA 95814
(916) 444-6670

California State World Trade
Commission
Export Finance Office
107 S. Broadway, Suite 8039
Los Angeles, CA 90012
(213) 620-2433

Export/Small Business
Development Center
110 E. Ninth Street, Suite A761
Los Angeles, CA 90079
(213) 892-1111

Export Import Bank
811 Vermont Ave. NW
Washington, DC 20571

Federation of International
Trade Associations
1851 Alexander Bell Drive
Reston, VA 22091
(703) 391-6108

Government of Quebec
Los Angeles Office
Patrice Lafleur
(310) 477-2217

Canadian Consulate
San Francisco Office
Consul General Percy Eastham
Economic Affairs—Stuart
Hughes
Cultural Affairs—Andrew
Thompson
(415) 495-6021

World Trade Center Institute
401 East Pratt Street, Suite 1355
Baltimore, MD 21202
(301) 576-0022

World Trade Centers
Association
One World Trade Center
55th Floor
New York, NY 10013
(212) 925-1400

International Advertising
Association
475 Fifth Avenue
New York, NY 10077

Los Angeles Chamber of
Commerce
International Commerce
Division
404 S. Bixel Street
Los Angeles, CA 90017

Mexican Chamber of Commerce
of Los Angeles
125 Paseo de la Raza, Room 404
Los Angeles, CA 90012
(213) 688-7330

Mexican Chamber of Commerce
of the United States
730 Fifth Avenue, 9th Floor
New York, NY 10019
(212) 333-8728

National Council on
International Trade
Documentation
350 Broadway, Suite 205
New York, NY 10013

San Diego Chamber of
Commerce
101 West C Street
San Diego, CA 92101

Shaw Direct Advertising
Chiapas 184-6
Colonia Roma Sur
Mexico, DF 564-0546

Texas Department of Commerce
P.O. 12728
Austin, TX 78711
(512) 472-5059

Trade Commission of Mexico
225 N. Michigan Avenue, Suite
708
Illinois Center
Chicago, IL 60601
(312) 856-0316
Offices also in: Dallas, Beverly
Hills, Atlanta

United States Commerce
Department
Exporter Counseling Division
Seminar Staff, Room 1099D
Washington, DC 20230

United States Council for
International Business
1212 Avenue of the Americas
New York, NY 10036
(212) 354-4480

United States Department of
Agriculture
14th Street and Independence
Avenue SW
Washington, DC 20250

United States—Mexico Chamber
of Commerce
1900 L Street NW, Suite 612
Washington, DC 20036
(202) 296-5198
515 S. Figueroa Street, Suite
1020
Los Angeles, CA 90071
(213) 623-7725

United States Small Business
  Administration
Small Business Development
  Center Program
409 Third Street, SW
Washington, DC 20416
(202) 205-7064

Woman's Business Advantage in
  Mexico
P.O. 133
8375 Leesburg Pike
Vienna, VA 22180

World Trade Center Institute
One World Trade Center
New York, NY 10048
(Publications)

World Trade Center of Orange
  County
1 Park Plaza, Suite 150
Irvine, CA 92714
(714) 724-9822

El Financiero
2300 South Broadway St.
Los Angeles, CA 90007
(213) 747-7547

World Trade
4199 Campus Drive
Irvine, CA 92715
(714) 725-0233

Export Today
P.O. 6072
Syracuse, NY 13127
(800) 825-0061

Twin Plant News
4110 Rio Bravo Dr.
El Paso, TX 79902
(915) 532-1567

U.S. Government Printing
  Office
Superintendent of Documents
Washington, DC 20402
(202) 783-3238

U.S. Department of Agriculture
International Trade
  Publications
Room 3420
14th and Constitution Avenue
  NW
Washington, DC 20230
(202) 377-5494

**TRADE SHOWS, FAIRS,
AND CONFERENCES**

Mexico Comexpo
Computers and technology
011 (525) 669-2215

International Book Fair
011 (525) 550-5716

Fonacot Fair
Trade Fair
011 (525) 553-3011

Expo Medica
Products and services for
  hospitals and laboratories
011 (523) 622-8790

M.I. Toys
Toy industry fair
011 (52-36) 208-41-97

Expo Lacetos
Milk machinery
011 (525) 574-4846

Transportation
Conference on transportation
(202) 296-3019

Expo Fresas
Agriculture and industry
011 (524) 626-4805

Expo Merceria
Clothing and textiles industry
011 (525) 554-8455

Expo Advertising
011 (523) 652-2663

Expo Fashion
011 (529) 925-3219

San Jose del Cabo Fair
Livestock and tourism
011 (525) 533-2175

Cement Fair
011 (528) 286-0020

Representaciones U.S.A.
011 (525) 591-0155

Flowers Fair
Flower-growing techniques
011 (527) 314-4322

A.N.T.A.D.
Supermarkets and department
   stores
011 (525) 254-1714

Expo Electrica
Industrial products
011 (525) 705-6341

Expo Electronica
National chamber of electronics
   industries
011 (525) 574-7411

International Exhibition on
   Tools and Machinery
011 (525) 604-8807

Hardware
011 (525) 591-0155

Annual Shoe Exhibition
011 (529) 972-0334

Leather and Shoe Exhibition
011 (52) 476-5800

Expo Textile
011 (523) 615-6646

National Sugar Fair
011 (521) 232-2924

Coffee Fair
011 (522) 816-2680

Expo Urbe Mexico
Urban services and supplies
011 5-682-5436

U.S.A. Expo
Machinery, equipment, and
   services
(800) 880-0048

LEGAL FIRMS

Baker & McKenzie
Chicago: (312) 861-1800
Dallas: (214) 978-3000
Los Angeles: (213) 629-3000
Miami: (305) 789-8900
New York: (212) 751-5700
San Diego: (619) 236-1441

Carlsmith, Ball, Wichman
Los Angeles: (213) 955-1236

Bryan, Gonzales, Vargas
Juárez: (16) 15-15-15
Mexicali: (65) 68-13-18
New York: (212) 682-3241
Mexico City: (5) 202-0096

Toney Anaya & Associates
New Mexico: (505) 988-5050

U.S. STOCK BROKERAGES FOR ADRs

Dean Witter Reynolds
Michele Lynch
(510) 746-2904

Merrill Lynch
Ted Fichter
(510) 866-2446

INDEX

ABOUT THE AUTHORS

Maggie L. Jessup

A fifth-generation Texan, Maggie Jessup was raised on the border in Laredo. She attended North Texas University and the University of Houston. Fluent in Spanish, Maggie lived in Mexico City for several years. Her sixteen years of experience with business in Mexico include work with General Motors, Goodyear, Bacardi, Chrysler, and Apple Computers. Maggie Jessup is a principal in an Atlanta-based import/export company as well as a director of the Jessup Group, a consulting organization specializing in United States/Mexico trade.

Jay M. Jessup

A fourth-generation Californian, Jay Jessup was brought up in Berkeley. He received a business degree from the University of Southern California and a law degree from Hastings College of Law. With seven years of experience in Mexican import and export, Jay now advises U.S. corporations doing business in Mexico and Mexican companies wishing to enter the U.S. market. A college-level instructor on the subject of conducting business with Mexico, an established national media expert, and a regular speaker on United States/Mexico trade, Jay Jessup is associated with the Jessup Group, an association of experts serving U.S. firms doing business in Mexico.

The Jessup Group
3232 Cobb Parkway
Atlanta, GA 30339
(404) 396-3080

276